tales of two cities

tales of two cities
a persian memoir
abbas milani

KODANSHA INTERNATIONAL
New York • Tokyo • London

Kodansha America, Inc.
114 Fifth Avenue, New York, New York 10011, U.S.A.

Kodansha International Ltd.
17-14 Otowa 1-chome, Bunkyo-ku, Tokyo 112, Japan

Published in 1997 by Kodansha America, Inc.
by arrangement with Mage Publishers, Inc.

First published in hardcover by Mage Publishers,
Washington, D.C., in 1996.
Contact Mage Publishers for translation rights.

This is a Kodansha Globe book.

Library of Congress Cataloging-in-Publication Data

Milani, Abbas.
    Tales of two cities: a Persian memoir / Abbas Milani.
        p.   cm. — (Kodansha globe)
    ISBN 1-56836-167-X (PB)
    1. Milani, Abbas.   2. Refugees, Political—Iran—Biography.
3. Iran—Exiles.   4. Iran—Politics and government—20th
century.   I. Title.   II. Series.
DS318.84.M55   1997
955.05'3'092—dc20
    [B]   96-46049

Manufactured in the United States of America on acid-free paper
97 98 99 00   BERT/B   10 9 8 7 6 5 4 3 2 1

*To my father,
and to the memory
of my mother*

The weight of this sad time we must obey
Speak what we feel, not what we ought to say
KING LEAR

tales of two cities

Ordeals of Exit

My flight was scheduled to leave Tehran at six in the morning and I had to be at the airport by midnight. I had to submit my passport to the Swissair offices even earlier—a full forty-eight hours before the flight—a security precaution, they claimed.

It was 1986. The war with Iraq was already six years old, the Revolution was only a few months older. Nocturnal missile attacks on Tehran had become routine. Iraq had even threatened to shoot down passenger planes in Iranian air space. For this reason, international airlines refused to fly to Tehran. Passengers had to be ferried by Iranian planes to a small airfield in the port city of Bandar Abbas, a short hop from Dubai. There, a safe distance from the reach of Iraqi fighters, foreign carriers would fly in, hurriedly pick up their passengers, and fly off to Europe or the Far East.

Around eleven o'clock that night I said good-bye to my son, Hamid. Leaving him behind, even though I knew it to be temporary, was the most tormenting aspect of my departure. When again we would meet, I did not know. Nevertheless, he slept with my promise of our imminent reunion.

Farewells to family and friends, many of whom I knew I would not see again, felt like witnessing or even participating in my own funeral, but bidding farewell to my aging parents was worse. I had gone to their house around eight. My mother, weakened by several strokes she had suffered over the last ten years, and my father, withering under the task of caring for her, both wanted to make the moment easier for me and valiantly tried to put on a happy face. Their casual banter could not hide the anxiety and sadness we all felt. I was the only one of their five children who was still living in Iran, and had become a more necessary component of their everyday life. Nevertheless, they had repeatedly urged me to leave the country. "You have a son to think of," they often said. But they were also thinking of me. A low grade fever of long duration and an erratic palpitation of my heart had already led to an angiogram and a false, but traumatic, diagnosis of lymphoma. These were, in fact, symptoms of the pressures of life in Iran. Bouts of depression had also begun to cast their long shadows over my everyday life. That night neither my parents nor I could bear a long good-bye. We kissed, and under an almost poisonous cloud of melancholy and guilt I left their home.

My wife was not going to take me to the airport. We said that we wanted her to stay with our son, but we both knew that was not the truth. Although my departure marked the beginning of our physical separation, our emotional estrangement was by then well established. Parviz Kalantari took me to the airport. I was bringing some of his paintings abroad with me to try to arrange for their sale.

Parviz arrived near midnight. I sank into the passenger seat of his car. Neither of us spoke, but with the turn of his ignition, tears began to roll down my face, and soon he too began to weep.

Few words were needed in the twenty-minute drive to the airport. The streets were deserted; there were road-blocks everywhere. Unlike other big cities where gangs, muggers, skinheads, and other predators have created and enforced a de facto state of siege, in Tehran the predators are the police. In Tehran one is, as a rule, free from the violence of the people but constantly wary of a variety of official forms of abuse.

Roadblocks were usually staffed by young men, many barely as tall as their guns. Every car was stopped. The drunkard, the romantic, the lecher, the political opponent—anyone or anything incongruent with a security officer's puny and punitive vision was what they sought to weed out. Before long, however, most people learned how to safely negotiate their way through this inquisitional labyrinth. Illicit lovers never traveled together, political activists rarely rode around at night, and those who had imbibed at a party would freshen their breath by chewing on a cucumber or some parsley before setting out.

By the time Parviz and I arrived at the airport, there was already a line at the entrance to the terminal. We quickly said farewell. We both had a long night of waiting ahead of us. Parviz had to make sure that I and his paintings would clear customs. In those days, there was no clear or predictable policy on who or what could leave the country. The whim of each official was the law of the moment. What they deemed appropriate was what one could take along—all else had to be left with the authorities for "safe keeping" or returned to a waiting relative or friend. Anyone even remotely familiar with the ethics of the Iranian bureaucracy opted for the latter—thus Parviz's wait.

The line through customs was agonizingly slow. Every piece of every passenger's luggage was inspected. Often a suspicious item—a backgammon board or a bulky frame—was dismantled lest there be inlays of gold, jewelry, or foreign currency. The last time I had gone through this line, about two years earlier, my son, Hamid, then only six, and his teddy bear of the same age, named Fatso, were also with me. Tired and tense from a long sleepless night punctuated only by short naps on our luggage or against one of my feet, Hamid held his bear in a tight embrace. A young man of about eighteen stood behind the inspection table. His long-sleeved baggy cotton shirt hung loosely over his trousers—as with women, so with men, no curvature of the body should, according to Islamic rules, protrude from beneath any article of clothing. His beard was scissors trimmed—orthodox Islam deems the roll of a naked blade on a man's face a frivolous pleasure, and Islam has no tolerance for frivolity. The young man glanced at the bear and said coldly, "That bear can not go." My appeals were of no avail, but Hamid's burst of tears and his unrelenting weeping finally softened the young man's heart. He merely slit the throat of the animal and poked through it, and then to my son's relief, allowed Fatso to come along. Afterwards, a friend in the United States stitched up the wounded neck. Yet the bear's proud upright gait was forever compromised.

As I waited in line, this time lonely and forlorn, I was aware that many of those leaving Iran that night had no intention of returning. They had to carry with them as many amenities of a future life and as much memorabilia of their emotional past as they could. Yet, extreme caution was more necessary. Save a few exceptions, most of these soon-to-be émigrés and exiles had no immigration visas from their countries of destination. They had to feign a short trip for leisure or business. Their luggage would become one of their devices of deception. If the contents of a bag suggested a permanent stay instead of a short sojourn, the authorities at the airports of destination could revoke even the visitor visa so diligently attained by the Iranian traveler.

The old man in front of me finally reached the inspection table, behind which loomed a tired ogre face in a drooping suit. The contents of the man's luggage were all spilled onto the table: pictures of his son, underwear, a few shirts, a crumpled suit, a pair of pajamas, and several

14

bags of pistachios. They were inspected item by item. Anyone near enough could see the man's belongings. For a society whose traditional Islamic architecture eschews windows in deference to *pardehs*, veils and enclosures, such openness seemed infamous to me. I felt humiliated not only because I witnessed it, but more so because I too docilely waited my turn to be thus exposed.

My half-empty single piece of luggage did not take long to ransack. I arrived at the ticket counter at about four-thirty in the morning. My confirmed reservation was, of course, no guarantee that I would in fact get a seat on the plane. There were few flights to Europe operating then, and tickets for such flights were much coveted. Inflation and avarice occasionally drove some airline employees to auction off reserved seats. But I was lucky.

With my boarding pass, I climbed the few granite steps to a large hall. To the left was a long, white marble-topped counter staffed by a reluctant sergeant of the city police, and behind him our passports that had been turned over to the airline offices forty-eight hours earlier, pigeonholed into alphabetized boxes. Every passenger wrote his or her name on a piece of paper and if the passport had not been confiscated by some government or paramilitary agency, the sergeant would retrieve it. I picked up mine, an officer at the end of the hall routinely stamped it, and then along with other passengers, I was herded into one of the two long gender-separate lines, each facing a row of hastily constructed cubicles.

Half an hour later, I stepped behind a gray canvas curtain into an area the size of a small car. A young man sat there, bearded, condescending, dressed in the green uniform of the Revolutionary Guards.

Pointing to the shelf, speaking in a monotone, he said, "Empty your pockets there. Leave your briefcase. Open your belt. Take off your shoes and your jacket."

I had heard about this ritual. A last rite of passage—yet I was still not ready.

His long hands frisked the whole of my body. I had heard that occasionally bodily orifices were searched for anal or vaginal caches. A "cavity search," in the parlance of the police. I was spared this. But the Guard leafed through my books and notes, examined the pads in my jacket, scrutinized the soles of my shoes. And all the while, he watched me out of the corners of his eyes. I guess he was looking for furtive glances, sweaty palms, or profuse perspiration. His curt "pick up your stuff" meant another stage in the ordeal of my exit was over.

In oppressive societies, where public opinion surveys

are prohibited, the one revealing exit poll is how eager people are to leave. Once we were finally on the plane and the doors had been shut, the anguish and despair so prominent on every face gradually gave way to lightness and the look of hope. Shortly after we were airborne, women began to visit the bathrooms. Veiled or scarved they walked in, and coifed and unveiled they emerged.

Though most of us were heading toward uncertain futures, leaving behind our emotional, cultural, intellectual, and at times even financial capital, we all seemed to be optimistic in our moment of departure. I was very conscious of our fortunate circumstance. In those days, to leave Iran legally was a luxury shared by a few and cherished by many. I myself knew of three middle-class families who in desperation had liquidated their assets and at great risk of police interception traveled to a border town. With the help of a guide cum trafficker, they then walked for forty-eight hours, children in one hand, and a life bundled in a piece of luggage in the other, crossing dangerous and inhospitable terrain infested with human and animal predators. They arrived in Pakistan or Turkey to uncertain futures, where hundreds of thousands of Iranians also waited and maneuvered for an entry visa to America or a West European nation.

Several months after my arrival in California, I received a letter from Parviz, who wrote about the night of my departure. He had waited at the airport till around six in the morning. He was sad. He had done a piece he called "your painting." The canvas, he wrote, was already on its way to America.

A long time elapsed and no canvas came. Finally it arrived in a bulky padded envelope from somewhere in Oklahoma. A short letter explained that the courier had been stranded in Turkey for six months, waiting for an entry visa into the United States. The canvas was folded over several times; it took much stretching on a cross to erase the creases it had incurred on its long journey. Such travails only foreshadowed its controversial life.

Before sending the canvas, Parviz had taken a picture of it, a copy of which ended up in the hands of a magazine editor. About a year after the death of Ayatollah Khomeini, emboldened by signs of liberalization and an impending "Tehran Spring," the editor decided to use the picture for the cover of an issue of his magazine, with the caption, "Will the exiles return?"

Hours after the magazine hit the stands, groups of veiled women, supported by the regime's paramilitary forces, stormed the office of the editor, claiming the picture was a direct insult to Islam, glamorizing the West and belittling the Revolution.

Revolutionary Guards eventually took the editor to prison and the controversy over the magazine grew. For several weeks, semi-official government newspapers engaged in a heated debate about the painting. The Minister of Islamic Guidance, in charge of censorship, was criticized by some clerics for tolerating blasphemy. He issued a proclamation explaining what he called the benign contents of the painting. Parviz was called to appear before a Revolutionary Tribunal. In his defense, he wrote an open letter assuring the critics that the painting contained no secret heretical or political code.

"A dear friend," he wrote in his published letter, "was leaving Iran. His mother was sick. He and I were sad for his departure. He entrusted me with the care of his ailing mother. His mother has since died. I doubt the friend will ever return home. That's the stuff of which the painting was made."

The center of the painting is the silhouette of a modern metropolis—colorful yet one-dimensional, a large amber-colored sun peeking through its skyscrapers. A glittery Eiffel Tower stands on the margins of the metropolis. A crayola-colored plane hovers above the city, while a bespectacled man, in modern dress, clings to the plane and floats with it like the tail of a kite.

At the bottom of the canvas, entombed in the black-veiled body of a mournful woman, stands a row of blue, brooding, beaten, and often windowless mud houses and mosques; a thin crescent of an azure moon flickers on the horizon. The bedazzled face of a young man looks on.

The canvas now hangs over my Sony television set alongside a small aquarium.

———————— Village Metropolis ————————

I was born in Tehran in 1948. I was seven before I ever heard of a birthday party and learned that the day and the month of birth are as important as the year. It took another decade and a trip across the world before I understood that for some people even the precise moment of birth, down to the seconds, and the corresponding constellation of heavenly bodies, is important. In my childhood, however, the only significant fact about our birth was the year—and that only to determine when we should go to school or be drafted into the army.

Once an ignoble village, pastoral and mountainous, Tehran is near the ruins of the historic city of Rey. Around the turn of the century, when the inhabitants of Tehran were ordered to stay home for forty-eight hours so that the first census could be taken, the population of the capital had already surpassed two hundred thousand. By 1948, one and a half million people lived in a city then caught in the jubilee and confusion of a short-lived postwar democracy.

When in 1975, after an absence of eleven years, I returned to the city of my childhood, it had swollen into an overcrowded, densely polluted, dangerously stratified, economically hyped, architecturally schizoid, dust-ridden modern metropolis, expanding away from its railroad tracks onto flattened layers of the mountainside.

When I left Tehran again, in 1986, it was a benighted city, endangered by nocturnal attacks of Iraqi planes, unraveling under the influx of war refugees from Afghanistan and the war-ravaged southern parts of Iran. It was economically enfeebled by an embargo, a war of attrition, and the flight of capital. The city was now mastered by zealots armed with guns and an infallible faith. They roamed the streets day and night, intent on creating a "new man" and a model new Islamic society.

As a metropolis, Tehran is an anomaly. Not only does the memory of its pastoral past—its winding labyrinthine alleys, its lack of a sewage system—encumber its expansion at every turn, it also lacks proximity to water. Seas and rivers are not just facilitators of trade, but also metaphors, mythically understood by humans, of openings, of journeys, of cleansing, of hope and utopia, and finally of fertility. Tehran has it's back to majestic mountains and its face to tormenting desert winds. It suffocates in the metaphor of its own geography.

I was born into a prosperous family. My father, like his father, was in the business of trade—steel from Belgium, crystals from Czechoslovakia, paper from Finland—but he has feigned poverty all his life. The education of his children was the only thing he was willing to spent lavishly on. In my childhood, embarrassed by his behavior, I attributed it to a miserly character. Later, dabbling in Iranian history helped uncover another possibility. In the past, the obviously wealthy were permanent prey to perennially poor and avaricious kings. In times of economic need, which was often, the king offered to spare the lives of the wealthy in exchange for their fortunes. It was an offer few chose to refuse. Of course, the pious kings were themselves wary of the wrath of the ultimate, omniscient, and vengeful King of the Heavens, and so they demanded that the transaction be performed with all the requisite religious sanctions. And thus it was that often, in the presence of a mullah, the assets of the unlucky men of wealth were ostensibly "sold" to the king in return for a cube of sugar.

My father's frugality with his capital contrasted sharply with my mother's extravagance with hers. Her family name was her most important asset. In a society where political connections are a form of social capital, my mother's pedigree of powerful ministers, senators, royal aides-de-camp, and one important writer was not to be lightly squandered. In spite of the strong patriarchal tradition of Iran, my mother kept, and occasionally flaunted, her maiden name all her life.

We lived on a street called Malek Shoaraye Bahar, in a neighborhood filled with literary and political luminaries. Our next-door neighbor, from whom my father had bought the land upon which our house was built, was Bahar, the most renowned and, some say, the last great classical poet of modern Iran. He was respected not only for his political valor and nationalist sentiments but also for his erudition and poetic genius.

Next to Bahar's house was the residence of the Honorable Golshaiyan. His name lived in infamy. He had been one of the principal signatories to a controversial agreement in 1952 that had returned the control of Iranian oil to a consortium of foreign companies. As a child, I knew little of his ignominy, but from the many police-escorted visitors to his house, I had an idea of his political importance.

Across the street from Golshaiyan's house was Qavam's garden, a lush and lavish orchard lined by towering poplars, setting off a graceful old mansion with heavy carved doors and beautiful stained glass windows. The house was often empty. The master usually lived in Shiraz, his permanent home, the seat of his feudal fiefdom.

A block away from our house sat the austere but expansive compounds of the American embassy. Not far from there, the Soviets occupied the palatial building of the old Russian tsarist envoys, and close by was the discreetly opulent British embassy. In Tehran, some of the best real estate has always belonged to foreigners.

By the time I left Tehran after the Revolution, the landscape of my childhood neighborhood had drastically changed. Our street, once lined with a wide stream and lush trees, now seemed emaciated. Where once was an orchard, the occasional residence of the aristocratic politician, there now stood slabs of cement stacked on steel scaffolds shadowed by a towering, immobile crane—the silhouette of a half-finished skyscraper, a memento of aborted dreams and designs. The original developer, notorious for his economic corruption and despised because he was a Bahai, had long since fled to Costa Rica.

The Honorable Golshaiyan's house was empty, the facade crumbling, the trees dying or dead. Bahar's house had long since been subdivided and sold into small residential units. Our house too, its beautiful brick facade now covered with faux marble, had been divided into six apartments. The once pristine walls of the American embassy were overwritten with political graffiti. A decidedly derelict building, an ominously naked flag staff, and dead or dying foliage was all that remained of the main embassy compound. In fact, in the old neighborhood, the only building whose facade and foundation had survived the years was where I went to elementary school.

While some of our teachers were nuns, the principal and proprietor was a French lay woman who sailed around the school in a heavy wheelchair, pushed by a servant and escorted by a big shaggy dog. A colorful embroidered quilt lay across her knees; she was always meticulously coiffured and exquisitely dressed. Madame Marika was her name, and so was the name of our school. It was a coeducational institution, an oddity in those days.

The principal had a commanding presence. Rumor had it that her jealous lover had shot her in a fit of passion. Her right hand, limp and disfigured by the bullet, slanted over the heart it had protected.

Our classes, except for about an hour a day, were conducted in French. In those days, a foreign language was a necessary staple in the diet of every child of the upper classes. While a few of my schoolmates were half-French, almost all were more conversant in French than in Persian. By the sixties and seventies, knowledge of a foreign language had become more and more an irreplaceable element of social status and mobility, while intimacy with Persian was disregarded, at times even disparaged.

I had been invited to a dinner party upon my return home in 1975, at which an uncle, then a deputy premier, was host. While such homecoming parties were part of a tradition of familial hospitality, they often also functioned as an arena in which connections were made, power and position were brokered, mates were matched, and deals were negotiated. As we sat sipping tea—for my uncle, though educated in Paris and secular in matters of politics, was deeply religious and refused to be party to the sacrilege of serving alcoholic beverages in his household—he called on two of his sons to be presented to the guests. To my great surprise, he talked to them not in Persian but in French, and when they spoke Persian, it was with a French accent.

Foreign languages had a hierarchy that changed with the changing landscape of Iranian politics. Before the Second World War, French was the language of eminence and culture; in the post-war years, English became the language of power, technology, and social mobility.

But language is power and power needs the legitimizing authority of language. When the language of a people is disdained by the elite in power, political eruptions cannot be far away. The Iranian political elite learned this the hard way—from the last shah himself.

In a land saturated with poetry and oration, the shah was no orator. The ineptitude of his spoken Persian undermined the aura of his authority. He was more articulate—if he could be said to be articulate at all—in French and English than in Persian. Whether talking to illiterate peasants or university professors, his tone was always haughty, but his discourse was invariably feeble, riddled with grammatical flaws. Yet the common lore of my childhood attributed mythic and omniscient qualities to the king. As children we debated with great zest and to no conclusive end whether he actually defecated and if so, whether it was golden or made of organic material.

Fear was also a cardinal element of pedagogy in my

childhood. If words can be said to have auras of meaning, then in those days the king had an aura of absolute authority, while father and mother conjured sentiments of love, reverence, and fear. Parental power was unequivocal. My father's authority was godlike. Although he never interfered in daily matters, we knew him to be the master of the house. We called him *Agha jan*, Dear Sir, or Dear Master.

The mores and manners of our household were designed to suit our parents' comfort and convenience. Children were necessary nuisances. When my parents took their siestas, all children, in spite of the restlessness of lazy summer afternoons and the temptations of the shimmering swimming pool, were banished to the back of the yard where they could not be heard. It was said that a good child is better seen than heard, and a good parent is better feared than loved.

Parenting was more primal and instinctive than cerebral then. Our generation of Persians has tried to apply a conceptual approach to child raising. We worry about the moral and psychological consequences of every gesture we make toward our children. The problem is particularly acute among those of us who, by force or choice, have ended up in exile. We lack the traditional authority of our parents, and the experience and nonchalance of our modern Western counterparts. Our ignorance about what an adolescent needs to survive in America further undermines our authority in the eyes of our children. In our childhood, we suffocated under patriarchy, and today, in our parenting days, we live under the tyranny of our children.

In my childhood, a hint of a grimace on the face of my parents or a new cadence in the tone of their conversation invoked a feeling of terror in me. And parents were not the only ones who used fear to shape and subdue children. My de facto parent, the man whom I called *Baba*, or father, a servant of two decades in our family, also occasionally relied on it. While my father spent his days with his business and my mother spent them at parties and gatherings, it was Baba who, day and night, and always with great affection, took care of me. Parental authority and the threat of physical punishment insured our fear of our parents. Baba, on the other hand, because of his social status, could not employ violence. To keep my mischief at bay, he had conjured an army of demons and dangerous child-devouring giants. The most dreaded demon of them all was called Lulu, a hunchback midget, who actually appeared, to my absolute horror, in our neighbor's attic. I was six when I finally learned that he was one of the neighbor's servants.

Schools, too, used fear as an instrument of social control. In those days physical punishments were routine, often inflicted in front of a whole frightened class or school. Even in our school, modern and liberal in its pretensions, where teachers factored in the possible displeasure of their students' powerful parents, certain humiliations were allowed. For instance, insolent students had to march around the schoolyard wearing a cardboard donkey hat.

But fear of God, king, parents, and teachers was not all that cast its shadow on my school years. Pederasty was another pestilence of those days. Not only did men of certain professions, like bicycle shopkeepers, truck drivers, and teahouse attendants, have a bad reputation, every stranger, we were told, was a potential predator. In seventh grade, when I first entered a public school, I learned with great disillusionment that even some teachers had designs on their students. There were many lurid tales. Some students bartered sexual favors for higher academic grades. I knew a young boy who sank so deep under an avalanche of guilt and chagrin over having succumbed, that he finally committed suicide. There were back-benchers in every class who defiantly whistled and

31

booed when a teacher began to flirt with a student. In ret-rospect, the atmosphere in some of those classes was vaudevillian, but at the time it was scary, not funny.

There were other times, though, when waves of jubi-lation washed away all traces of fear and melancholy. *Nowruz* was the best time of the year. A quintessential classical Persian ceremony, celebrated for several millen-nia and undaunted by a variety of historical adversaries, including the Islamic Republic which has tried to brand it as a relic of pagan Persia, *Nowruz* marks the vernal equinox and is embroidered with many rich rituals.

It was at this time each year, when the snow began to melt and flowers began to bloom, that my sister and I would find a quiet corner of the house and, with all the solemnities of a yearly ritual, count our "happinesses." The new year also meant a visit to the tailor. Custom has it that on the moment of the vernal equinox, at least one piece, or preferably all of a person's clothing, must be new. But nego-tiating a new suit of our liking was no easy matter. First there were parental strictures on the color of the fabric we could choose. Too light a color was considered gaudy and frivolous. Too dark was too somber. The apparel, my fam-ily firmly believed, "oft proclaims the man."

We bought the fabric from a shop in the bazaar. Always

a seat of power and wealth in Tehran, the bazaar was a series of brick and mud dome-covered, open arcades, through which shafts of light filled with dancing dust illuminated the densely populated walkways. Organized by trade in the fashion of medieval towns, the bazaar was at its bustling best around *Nowruz*—until the sixties and seventies and the growth of modern shopping.

Another sign of *Nowruz* was the housecleaning that preceded it, the Iranian equivalent of spring cleaning when old men, often as bent as the big bows they carried on their backs, roamed the streets, hawking their indispensable service with an incomprehensible high-pitched call. We called them cotton beaters. They removed the cotton stuffing of pillows, mattresses, and quilts, and then with their bow, a wooden mallet and a tall wooden stick, beat out the accumulated dirt and dust of a year.

Rugs and curtains, windows and walls were washed and dusted in anticipation of the moment when even nature would put on a new face. Cleaning the walls was easy. I remember them hauntingly barren. If there were any household adornments, these were usually antique bowls, lamps and plates. Paintings were a rarity. For a while, a couple of my older brother's still lifes hung in our living room. Except for its miniatures, ours was a society all but bereft of a tradition of representational painting.

And then came the rituals of the last Wednesday of the year. Its theme was pyro-purification of soul and fate. We jumped over small bonfires lit in backyards and sidewalks, singing a song that promised to leave for the fire all that was yellow in life, and partake of the vigor and vitality represented by the red of the flame.

During my childhood, the Wednesday celebration was a cherished harbinger of *Nowruz*; after the Islamic Revolution, the same ritual took on a new political meaning. The Islamic regime saw it as a remnant of pagan fire-worship. For the unhappy populace, continuing the celebration became a relatively safe gesture of defiance against the new regime. Pitched battles, combining the jocularity of a carnival and the passionate intensity of a serious war of symbols, were fought between armed Revolutionary Guards and young and old citizens of the city. Such struggles provided the subdued population with a sense of meaning and resistance. Sometimes it seems as if totalitarianism can only be undermined by cultural wars of attrition. Our celebrations of the last Wednesday of the year had become an important battle in that war.

About an hour to the moment of *tahvil*, when the new year would begin, our family, freshly attired, gathered around the *haft seen* table. *Haft* means seven in Persian, and *seen* is the *s* of our alphabet. The *haft seen* arrangement must include seven items whose Persian names begin with an *s*. In all families, the seven objects are commonly the same. How refined and exquisite the containers for these items are is an important gauge of each family's social status. A glass jar with some gold fish, a mirror, a volume of the Koran, and in more modern households, a collection of Hafez's poems often accompany the arrangement. In our house, my mother's most precious antique glazed enamel Chinese bowls with gold rims and elaborate designs, her most exquisite *termes*, or fine hand-woven fabrics, her coveted long-stemmed tulip lights, were all saved for our yearly *haft seen* table. Even the best radio programs were reserved for the hours before the change of the year.

Just before the end of the year, while the rest of the family gathered around the *haft seen* table, my mother and sister made their customary visits to every room of our house. My mother carried a Koran in one hand and a dish full of *noghl* in the other. *Noghl* is a favorite Persian confection, and those used for the new year had been taken to a holy shrine and blessed, and so had become graced relics. My sister carried a tulip light in one hand and a lighted candle in the other. My mother opened the door to each room, hummed litanies in Arabic, believed by Moslems to be the language of God; blew the air thus blessed by godly verses into each room; and dropped a piece of *noghl* behind each door—all in the hope of bringing good fortune to that room for the coming year.

The solemn shot of a cannon heralded the arrival of the new spring. A tidal wave of joy broke what had felt like an eternity of silence and waiting. Greetings and kisses were exchanged, beginning with my father and mother, down a ladder determined by age. Tradition had it that the face you first gazed on after the vernal equinox would determine the tidings of the new year. Some faces were bad omens, others delivered good fortunes for the year. My mother was said to have a good face. Each year, my father insisted on opening his eyes to my mother's good face.

After the greetings came the gifts. Only parents and elders were expected to give gifts to children, and to our great joy, the most customary gift in those days was money. Minutes after the dawn of the new year, traditional visits to relatives and friends began. A whole labyrinth of rules and expectations had developed around the order and duration of these new year visits. Rarely a year passed when someone's sense of social and family status and pride was not hurt by what she or he perceived to be a too short or too late visit. But as children we were usually oblivious to these tensions and only relished the fact that schools were closed, cash and delectable homemade confections abounded, and we got to see our favorite relatives.

Next to summer, *Nowruz* was when I could spend the most time with my childhood sweetheart. All of my life I have loved to be in love and it all began with my cousin. In societies wary of premarital and even prepubertal gender mixing, emotional incest is inevitable. Much of our time together was spent playing in make-believe movies. We were, I think, the first generation of Iranians whose sense of reality, morality, and aesthetics was at least partially shaped by cinema. I, a film addict, often directed our love-spun movies and managed to work many kissing scenes into the script.

Our generation's nickelodeons were light tinsel boxes, heavily ornamented and carried on the shoulders of old men who roamed the streets, enticing children to glimpse into their wondrous machines. These mobile and primitive magic lanterns were called *Shahr-e Farang*, or "European city." In return for a small coin, we peeked at illuminated postcard images of far away places.

Soon French, American, Italian, and Indian films began to arrive. There was no dubbing in those days. Every few minutes, the action stopped and a paragraph in Persian with the bare plot outline of the unfolding events filled the screen; usually a voice read out the inscriptions. Then dubbing became a fad, and John Wayne began to speak in the street slang of Tehran, and the Japanese commander of the camp in *The Bridge on the River Kwai*, for some odd reason, could only speak a broken Persian.

Cinema was where I learned the little I knew about the language of love. When my cousin, coquettish and reticent at the same time, complained about the saturation of our make-believe films with kisses, I invariably deferred responsibility, assuring her that, "In the cinema, it is always like this."

All the children in our family had one favorite uncle whom we saw a lot of during the *Nowruz* holidays. His name was Nasser. Though he was forty, he talked with the honesty and innocence of a young boy. To our delight, he also peppered his conversation with light profanities. He had the memory of a savant, prodigious in its power, though often trivial in its content. He could remember the license plates and the phone numbers of every friend and relative. He also knew many lines of poetry by heart. In fact, he fancied himself a poet. His forte was satire. Repetition of numbers, of anecdotes, of poems was a staple of his conversation.

We and others in the family thought him saintly. We believed his prayers were always answered, and for the right compensation, he would pray for our success in an exam or the favorable resolution of other dilemmas we faced.

For many years, his preoccupation was time. In those days, he asked only for a watch as the price for his prayer. He wore each watch for a while and then with a pestle, flattened it in a mortar. Then he went through a calendar fetish. He carried, in a bundle, thousands of small neatly cut pieces of paper, all ostensibly to be used for a calendar he was going to write but never did. While all the children loved him and craved his company, his powerful brothers, embarrassed by his strangeness and frightened of what he might say in a crowd, tried to keep him banished for as much of the year as possible. Often they kept him on the move between cities, on small errands that were no errands, a twentieth-century version of a medieval ship of fools.

In my childhood years, madness was considered a curse, not a malady, a source of embarrassment, something to be denied, quarantined, and sequestered. I remember my mother and other philanthropist ladies make their monthly visit to Tehran's only lunatic asylum, where they distributed cigarettes and confections amongst the patients. Yet, in spite of the social stigma of madness, my uncle's occasional visits brought gaiety and lightness to our lives, particularly around *Nowruz*.

Our two-week new year holiday was over and it was time to return to school too soon, particularly for me, a mediocre student in a family where academic excellence seemed the precondition for survival. The whole world, animate and inanimate, constantly reminded me of the achievements of my sister, my brothers, and my cousins, and simultaneously berated my dismal failings. My problem had become especially acute after I flunked the first grade. I was miserable in math. I remember how shocked my teacher was, and how chagrined and frightened I became when she, sarcastically disbelieving, went over my final exam wherein I had multiplied a two-digit number by another two-digit number and arrived at an eight-digit result. But those days in Iran, every problem save political transgressions against the regime could be solved with the right connection or sufficient capital.

The first day of my second year of school, with the

eight-digit figure buzzing around my head, I had resigned myself to the most inconspicuous place in the nervous line of incoming first graders. As we waited for the commencement of the morning ritual of prayers, singing of the national anthem, and our morning dose of advice, reproofs, and threats, I saw my mother arrive. Perfectly dressed, her black leather purse authoritatively tucked under her arm, she strode into the principal's office. Near the end of the ceremony, she emerged from Madam Marika's bureau and with an unforgettable gesture that combined admonishment for my failure, pride at her own triumph, and compassion for my plight, she motioned me to join the line of second graders.

With the help of private tutors, who often conveniently happened to be my class teacher for the year, and inspired by a desire to avoid, at any cost, another experience with the sweltering sensation of that motherly gaze, I never failed another course in my life. But there was something else that made my next four years at that school uncomfortable.

In those days, public schools in Iran required all students to have a crew cut. Apparently there was both a hygienic as well as a political reason for this; most students in those days took a shower a week at best. All children dreaded catching ringworm. Indeed, my own

41

younger brother had become infected, ominous patches of a white crust appearing in several places in his hair. I remember the summer day of his cure.

He sat outside near the swimming pool, close to large clay pots full of jasmine. His hair was to be removed by a process normally used as a depilatory technique by women. An attendant with nimble fingers placed each strand of undesired hair between two crisscrossed sturdy strings, and with a precise, quick yank of the strings, uprooted the strand. My poor brother's whole head was to be thus shorn of hair. Then a cloth soaked in an adhesive concoction of raw eggs and other herbs was attached to the inflamed but hairless head. After twenty minutes, in spite of the patient's heart-wrenching cries, the cloth was pulled off. This treatment was repeated three times. To avoid it, a crew cut seemed a paltry price to pay.

I think crew cuts also have a political function. Masters of authoritarian institutions all seem to understand the psychological effect of short hair. Samson lost his powers with the loss of his hair. Inmates in prisons, soldiers in the army, and students in the public schools of my childhood would, the masters hoped, lose their powers of defiance with the loss of their hair.

While my school had a liberal hair policy, my parents

did not, and to my constant consternation, they forced me to wear a crew cut, which was not required of my classmates. In every class picture I have of my elementary school years, I stand out sorely amongst the well-groomed heads of the other boys and girls.

In seventh grade, I entered a public high school where my short hair was no longer an oddity. But I felt estranged and out of place for other reasons. The new milieu was incomparably tougher than the small protected atmosphere of my previous school and demanded new strategies of survival. I had to give up French and learn English. I had to contend with another breed of classmates. There were the old-timers who each had taken several years to pass a grade. Most had long ago begun to shave, a fact in itself awe-inspiring to the rest of us. The elder students not only lorded it over us, but even intimidated most of our teachers. Where they congregated was a danger zone few dared enter.

All my attempts to put on a face to cope with the new faces came to nothing because of my parents' insistence that my Baba walk me to and from school every day. It was particularly embarrassing in this tough public school. I negotiated a compromise with Baba, whereby he would walk inconspicuously across the street. But it was not enough to save me from the stigma of being overly pampered and protected.

Of course my parents' protectiveness did not discourage them from sending me abroad when I was fifteen and a half years old. A Western education was a hope of every Iranian student and the fate of almost all children of the upper classes. Yet I was hurled into my fate with little premonition and almost no preparation. I had never so much as walked without a chaperone to my school, only a few short blocks away from our house. Yet on June 14, 1964, my father gently pulled me away from the tearful embrace of my mother, and with the sobs of my sister in our ears, walked me past customs and, himself discreetly damp-eyed, handed me to a waiting stewardess from British Airways. She hung a sign around my neck indicating my status as a minor traveling alone and led me to my seat, and thus began my lonely flight to America.

*A picture of my maternal grandfather with his
four sons, he remained a cleric all his life.*

*My paternal grandfather sitting in the middle
with my father standing in front of him.*

*My maternal grandfather again with his sons,
who became secular politicians.*

My father (top left), with his brother and a cousin.

My father in Baku.

My paternal grandmother with my father and aunt.

*My mother and father at the time of
their wedding in June 1939.*

My family and I (lower left corner). The figure on the far right is the only image I have of my Baba.

My older brother Hossein and my sweetly mad uncle.

*Second grade class photo at Madam Marika's.
I'm second from the left in the third row.*

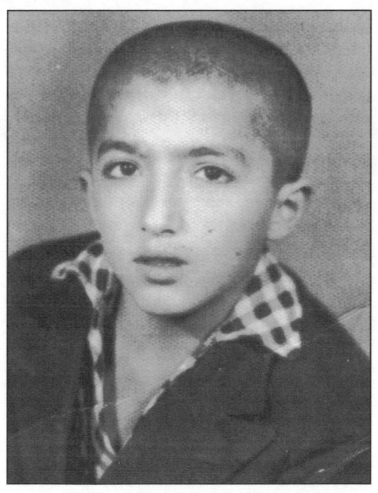

My picture in my first year of high school.

My son and I in 1985.

Temptations of the Soul

My childhood was contaminated with religion. The kind of playfulness that, as a rule, defines the experience of childhood was squandered by the fear of transgressing Lordly edicts that were part of every facet of life. While in Christianity man is thought to be the son of God, I was born into a religion in which I was Allah's *bandeh*, the Persian equivalent of a servant or slave. Shiism, the state religion of Iran, sacramentalizes all aspects of daily life. It has answers and strictures for every conceivable, and sometimes even inconceivable, question. From personal hygiene to major philosophical queries, from problems of banking to the correct Islamic style of sneezing and the proper prayers to be thence recanted, all are covered in the Book, and to ignore the Book is to court the dangers of hell, meticulously laid out with all the details of suffering. Life in those years seemed like walking on egg shells beneath which gaped the abyss of eternal suffering.

Religion was synonymous with mourning and fear; with an angel on each shoulder, pen and ledger in hand, observing, assessing, and recording every deed and every thought as a debit or a credit toward the day of reckoning and a bottom line of virtue or sin. At the same time, the timbre of my religious experience was also shaped by my nanny who tried to cure the piercing pain in my ears by murmuring Arabic litanies near my earlobes and then blowing the sanctified air into my ears. Religion in those days was synonymous with incomprehensible rituals, occasionally violent, often filled with the pungent odor of body sweat and of an ill-scented rose water that had a depressingly long afterlife. In religious ceremonies, the scented water was splattered on the faces and the bodies of every mourner. To shun the splatter, we were told, was a defiant act. God, they implied, disdained those who did not smell like the rest of the flock.

Religion conjured images of bearded, ogre-faced, turban-headed clerics who laundered the laws of an ever-vengeful God and fostered His ingenious punishments of hell and His promises of carnal and gastronomic pleasures in heaven. Hell frightened me and heaven was incomprehensible.

Under the constant mourning and the cult of martyrs, there was also a carnival subtext in Shiite rites. For our family, the month of mourning was also when we traveled to our uncle's house in the country, and the promise of childish games and gaiety in a sea of languishing adults.

Philosophers have said writing is a *pharmakon*, a cure and a curse, a poison and an antidote. The same can be said of religion in Iran. It has caused much anguish, yet it has often provided comfort to the souls it has hurt. It has been, historically, a cardinal element in legitimizing oppression; at the same time, almost invariably, all Iran's movements of social protest have been religious in their origins or pretensions.

Though my family was not particularly religious, the landscape of my childhood was dominated by religion. Of course as they aged, my father turned more stoic and my mother more religious, hoping, like most of the elderly, to parlay a belated piety into eternal bliss. But in my youth, the only regular religious ritual of our household was a weekly visit by a blind mullah, Sheik Hossein. He arrived every Friday around ten in the morning, with his son as his guide. The son came to a tragic end when the Islamic Republic accused him of membership in a radical religious group and sent him to the firing squad.

Sheik Hossein would descend on a wooden chair, in the middle of an empty room. His only occasional audience was one of the servants. For as long as I remember, he repeated the same story that began as a moralizing sermon and soon became an elegy of Imam Hossein, the quintessential martyr of Shiism. By then the monotony of his conversational tone had surged into an abrasive mournful cant. Many Shiite clerics have been vocalists of considerable talent; indeed some of Iran's best known singers began their careers as reciters of the Koran. The many similarities that exist between modes *(dastgahs)* of classical Persian music and modes used in mourning cants have facilitated this transition. But Sheik Hossein was no vocalist. When I asked my mother why the blind mullah was paid to sing and deliver a sermon to an often empty room, she responded, "Good omens and a good name come to the house regularly visited by a man of God."

There was also fasting in the month of Ramadan. In those days my mother and the servants were the only household members to fast. From dawn to dusk, as religious laws required it, there was to be no eating, drinking, vomiting, fornicating, masturbating, hubris against

God, the prophet, his progeny and their successor, no immersing of heads in water and, finally, no enemas. Like medieval Europe in times of Lent, public acts betraying a broken fast were, and still are, punishable by law. My grandmother used to say God has ordained the fasting season to educate the rich about the travails of the poor; human compassion through simulated hunger. More modern proponents of Islamic rituals discovered and lauded the dietary and biological genius of the fast— an internal cleansing, a heaven-designed respite for the tired body, a moment of God's perennial medical wisdom.

Whatever the original impulse, fasting had by the time of my childhood taken a slightly different bent—at least for the rich. A sumptuous meal was consumed before dawn. A lore had developed around the best dietary strategies for sustaining a day's hunger and thirst. A raw egg was recommended as the best "closer." My mother slept away most of her fasting days.

And then a delicious meal was prepared for dusk. Some of the best delicacies of Persian cooking were set aside for the most serene meals of my childhood. Prepubescent children were not required to fast, but we did join in the sumptuous meals that were prepared every night. As we sat around the table, our giant Telefunken radio played beautiful recitals of Islamic litany. Then the countdown began; at the precise moment of sunset, with the recital of Koranic verses, the meal commenced. A sweetened tea was the recommended opener.

Two of the rare delicacies of those days, were *zulbia* and *bamieh*, made of yogurt, honey, sugar, flour, and saffron, baked in small bite-size morsels or flat pieces with beautiful floral designs. In spite of their enormous popularity, these confections could only be found in the month of fasting. It was even believed that a mighty king had once said, "I hope Ramadan comes sooner so we can eat some *zulbia*."

In the early seventies, in the month of Ramadan, a friend of mine, an economist by vocation and avocation, tried to purchase a bit more *bamieh* than *zulbia*. He was about to learn his first serious economic lesson on the nature of capitalism in societies like Iran where consumer sovereignty has no place, and the tyranny of retailers reigns supreme. The shopkeeper replied angrily, "That's impossible," and complained, "Everybody asks me the same thing." My friend ventured a recommendation, "Since the price is the same, why don't you make more *bamieh* than *zulbia*?" By then disgusted by my friend's temerity, the man answered curtly, "Because that's the way we have always done it."

In short, even utilitarian laws of economics succumb to the force of tradition. It took the entrepreneurial genius of the exiled Iranian cottage industry to make the confections not only available all year round, but in any proportion desired.

The delights of Ramadan were overshadowed by a perpetual mood of mourning. Shiism, in principle, denigrates joy. Laughter, they used to tell us, is the work of the devil. According to Ayatollah Khomeini, Islam survives by the weeping of the pious. A most reliable *Hadith*, the authoritative narratives from the words or the deeds of the Prophet and his progeny, even promises absolution from all mortal and venial sins in return for tears shed for the martyrs of Shiism.

The frenzy of this cult of grieving reaches a zenith in the month of Moharam. Whole cities and villages drape themselves under a black veil. From the first day to the tenth, reaching a climax on the noon of Ashura (the tenth), processions in black, organized by neighborhoods or trades, take to the streets. Men flagellate their naked chests to a crimson color, or whip their bare backs with a chain into a blue blistering bruise, continuously chanting elegies to Hossein, martyred in the battle of Karbala in the year 680. Women and children crowd the sidewalks, one a chorus of weeping, the other foot-soldiers of this bizarre carnival. Even in religious ceremonies, traditionally a rare public arena dominated by women, when men enter the stage, women are marginalized.

Each procession carries elaborately designed banners, flags, and insignias printed with Koranic verses, adorned with symbols of mourning and martyrdom. In those days, piety was a social capital and not only individuals but also neighborhoods vied for more and more spiritual affluence.

Occasionally, there were processions wielding machetes. The government had officially decreed such forms of mourning illegal, but often looked the other way when they appeared on secluded streets or neighborhoods. I first encountered such a parade when I was about six. Early one morning on a Moharam stroll with my Baba, we heard the frenzied shouts of "Hossein, Hossein." As we turned the corner, instead of the normal ebony-clad flagellating procession I had expected, I saw, to my bewilderment and terror, a circle of about fifty men draped in white blood-stained shrouds, machetes in hand, the "agony of a trance" on their faces, spasmodically jabbing their blood-gushing foreheads. Frightened, I turned to hide my face in the old man's embrace and implored him to take me away. With his gentle voice now punctuated with occasional sobs, he told me of the recompense set aside not only for those who, in their lamentation, take a sword to their own heads, but also to those who witness such sacred moments of sacrifice.

When we finally parted from the scene, I asked the old man about the sword wielders' secret of survival. "It's a miracle," he said, "it happens every year. God protects them, otherwise they'd all be dead."

Later I learned that the sword wielders first gather in a designated enclosed place, and begin a long frenzied cant. Concurrent with the cant, they tap their foreheads with the width of the machete, repeating the act long enough for the site of the future cuts to become, for all practical purposes, anesthetized. There was also a certain mastery required to ensure that the machete hits the forehead at a precise angle. A wrong angle of contact could mean death or permanent injury, as it did too often every year.

The sight of that zealotry frightened me as a child and continues to haunt me as an adult. In 1975, at the height of the modernizing putsch, I returned to Iran and saw throngs of mourners with faces that spoke of poverty and pastoral hardships wielding their chains, rhythmically flagellating, chanting their praise of Imam Hossein as the King of all Kings and the herald of salvation. As they passed in front of Tehran's modern skyscrapers and exquisite nightclubs and boutiques, I knew that a volcano was ready to erupt. More than anyone else, Ayatollah Khomeini recognized the incipient volatility of this dormant force. He successfully channeled that strong undercurrent of frustration and fanaticism into the politics of resentment—the pivot of all revolutions, according to Nietzsche. When the volcano erupted, piece by piece an image of our society began to emerge that was a surprise to even the most pessimistic observer. In a sense, the Islamic Revolution was the Iranian body politic in a frenzy of flagellation and self-inflicted wounds.

The body has always been an obsession of Shiism. It is a tempter of the soul, an instrument of Satan. It must be veiled, punished, and reined in. Shiism disparages the body. It strictly prohibits the gaze of men and women on the body of the other. Even gazing upon one's own body is disdained. There are religious strictures against husbands and wives engaging in a naked embrace. Once I even read a *Hadith*, next to the Koran the most authoritative source of Islamic law, that claimed baldness would come to any man who gazes at a woman's genitals. Nearly all Persian men and women I have come to know have been ill at ease with their own bodies and its nakedness.

I remember my own first tango when I was sixteen. The close embrace of my partner, in spite of the heavy starch on her rented gown, gave me an erection. I pulled back, ashamed. It was only when I was forty that I mustered enough courage to ask the sweetheart of my middle years whether it was aesthetically acceptable for American men to have erections while dancing. "Not only is it acceptable," she said, "its absence is almost a sign of malice." A Persian friend told me that in his post-adolescence, when he went dancing, he tied his penis against his belly.

All forms of autoeroticism and homosexuality are also seriously restricted and denigrated. Homosexuality was, in the old regime, always punishable under the law; under the Islamic Republic it is punishable by death. Masturbation, we were told, weakened the eyesight, reduced virility and fertility, caused acne and nervous tics, and led to premature baldness.

While these inhibitions gnawed away at my corporeal self-orientation, I realized the depth of their psychic scars during my first experience with a professional masseuse. It was a Valentine's gift from Barbara, and I was about forty years old.

She was Russian by birth, a dermatologist by profession, and a masseuse out of the necessities of exile. Her books on French Impressionism, her selection of exquisite pieces by Bach and Albinoni, her intimacy with *The Master and Margarita* ("one of the few books I brought with me," she said), and her delight that I had translated the novel into Persian, the many icons decorating the walls, all testified to her unique cosmopolitanism—at once cultured and pastoral. Yet, all the while during the massage, I found myself painfully conflicted. Puritanical and prudish inclinations about the body, both relics of my past, seemed at odds with the pleasureful touch of a strange woman. Indeed, every element of that encounter was inimical to Shiite rules. The body must be particularly guarded from the contamination of the *najes*, the unclean.

And the "unclean" meant everyone other than Shiites. I learned this on the first Omar Festival of my life. A couple of weeks before the occasion, a scarecrow-like effigy, disturbingly disfigured and ugly, made out of the most filthy material found in our household, was constructed and placed in the malodorous outhouse in the back of our yard. As if such an exile was not enough of a punishment, the effigy was vilified and spat upon at every turn, and then on the night of the festival, my mother, singing songs disparaging to Omar and his followers, set the effigy on fire. The mood around that bonfire of vanity was boisterous and jovial. When I asked my mother who Omar was, she quickly responded, *"Yek sag-e Sunni,"* a Sunni dog.

For us, Islam was synonymous with Shiism, and then there were those paltry and pathetic followers of Omar. Shiism was said to be the religion of the Prophet and his progeny, while Sunnis were the cursed followers of those who had usurped the mantle of the Prophet. It took me years to discover that Shiites are indeed a small minority in the Muslim world; that Omar was the most influential figure in Islamic expansion and a central architect of what is considered the "golden era" of Islamic culture; that much blood has been shed in the history of Iran in sectarian feuds that pitted the Sunnis against the Shiites; that many of Iran's most revered literary icons of the past had been Sunnis; and finally that a key to the historic survival of Shiism has been its pivotal belief that the truly pious are always a minority.

Some later-day analysts have seen this "Omarphobia" as a form of sublimated nationalist sentiment. It was Omar, they say, who forced the curse of Islam on the Zarathustrian soul of Persia. According to these historians, the paisley, so prominent in Persian artifacts, is a metaphor for the bent and subdued pine tree that was the symbol of Zarathustra. It was Omar who forced Islam on

Iran and turned the upright gait of the pine into the curved posture of the paisley.

If the specter of religious intolerance had been limited only to the Sunnis, then such nationalist arguments might have been more plausible. But in fact Jews, as well as other religious minorities, were also victims of spiritual sectarianism. Jews were people to avoid. I was frightened by them; child abductors they were, who used their victims as ingredients in demonic rituals. There was the Passover bread, baked with the blood of a Muslim child, whirling in a circle of Jews, daggers behind their backs, beguiling smiles on their faces. Jews, we were told, hung the innocent Muslim children from a hook atop a burning fire, and gradually extracted their human oil and used it as ingredients of a "Jewish soap." At the same time, Jews were synonymous with squalor and malodor. I was well into my thirties when a barber, nodding after an affluent-looking departing customer, told me in a confidential tone, "I don't like working on their hair, but what can we do, they have the money." And, "Who are they?" I asked. "Jews." And, "How do you know?"

"They have a particular smell."

When our rooms were in a mess, my mother would admonish us, "What is this, a Jewish neighborhood?" And indeed in the earlier part of the century, there had been an exclusively Jewish ghetto in Tehran where most of the city's Jews lived. My grandmother once even boasted of the good old days when Jews had to wear a little flag when they left their neighborhoods, "On rainy days, they couldn't leave their area; a wet Jew is particularly *najes*. And they never dared use a Muslim public bath."

In the Persian lexicon, there are several names for Jews: *Kalimi, Mussavi, Jahudi* and *Johud*, or the Jew, the one most often used in the vernacular. As an adjective, *Johud* was pejorative with connotations of miserliness, blood-phobia, and cowardice. Once when a new teacher was calling roll in our class, my halfhearted response caused her to ask, "Why do you talk like a Jew?" I began to weep, though for a fourth grader, weeping was a girlish thing to do. The affront, recounted to my parents, was serious enough to warrant a rare visit by my mother to the principal's office and the teacher's subsequent explanation to the class that her comment was meant to be a joke.

Not only the vernacular, but even Persian prose and poetry, from the classics to modern masterpieces of literature, are embarrassingly littered with sometimes subtle, often crude jibes at the Jew.

Ironically, while much of the world has chastised the

Jews for what Hannah Arendt calls the Jewish "non-assimilationist," self-adulating sense of being "the chosen people," the Shiites, convinced of their own elite status amongst the believers, have always been wary of Jewish assimilation into Muslim territory.

Yet another difference between the anti-Semitism and its Persian counterparts is that in modern Europe, anti-Semitism has been largely a secular ideology portraying Jews as architects of social, aesthetic and moral decadence, the source of socialist ideas as well as the evils of finance capital. But the Jews' essential social guilt in Iran, aside from not being Muslim, has been the promotion and perpetuation of usury. Unlike its European counterpart, anti-Semitism in Iran has not been used as a political instrument to seize or wield power and liquidate the Jews. Instead, it has been used to marginalize them from society and keep them spiritually subdued.

In the late seventies, with the imminent rise of the Islamic Republic, tens of thousands of Iranian Jews opted for a quick exit, taking their sometimes substantial professional, entrepreneurial, and financial capital with them. Those who by choice or necessity remained in Iran received ostensible legal protections but were, nevertheless, subjected to chronic intimidation and discrimination.

Soon after the Revolution the freedom of Jews to travel was curtailed. Every Jew who desired an exit visa had to provide, as collateral, the passports of two other Jews under the age of thirty. An office was discreetly set up to "supervise" the problem of Iranian Jewry. I only became aware of its existence because of the travails of a friend.

An eminent scholar, teaching and researching at one of the world's foremost universities, he was invited by the government to lead a seminar in Iran. He came gladly. Departure was another matter. He described long inter-rogations; as a Jew, he was assumed to be a Zionist, and the burden of disproof was on him. The interrogators wanted to know everything about every member of his family, and particularly those who had migrated to Israel. My friend converted to Islam. His inquisitor, the twenti-eth-century version of the infamous Torquemada, doubted the sincerity of his conversion and berated it as an act of "bad faith." My friend constantly talked to me about his son, whom he had never seen and was by then already three years old. He despaired at the growing impatience implicit in his English wife's letters. The last I heard of him, he was looking for a connection with whose help he hoped to escape Iran on foot and head for the hills, his son, his wife, and his research.

But it has been the Bahais, and not the Jews, who have been the true modern nemesis of Shiism in Iran. Originating in the turmoil preceding the Constitutional Revolution of 1905, the Bahai faith has been essentially a middle-class phenomenon. Its promise of world peace and international brotherhood, its preoccupation with the moral education of humans away from the arena of politics, and its call for equality are reminiscent of the Rousseauian civic religion so popular around the time of the French Revolution. But ever since I can remember, the Bahais have been subjected to every conceivable political abuse, and sometimes to serious physical attacks as well. In the mid-fifties, when I was about nine years old, I witnessed the jubilation of a frenzied mob, goaded and herded by a mullah, as they ransacked the most sacred Bahai temple in Tehran.

Beginning in the sixties, the torment of the Bahais subsided dramatically, to be rekindled with a new gusto after the victory of the Islamic Revolution. Bahais were said to be the cohorts of Zionism, instruments of Free Masonry, itself the bane of modern Iranian politics. For instance, they were presumed to have created SAVAK, the much despised secret police of the last ruling monarch. Their disinclination toward politics was believed to be a facade

74

for political espionage and part of a grand design to win dominance in Iran, and ultimately the world. We learned that their alleged agents, including Abbas Hoveyda, prime minister of Iran for thirteen years, had infiltrated every strata of power in the country. In fact, Bahai hegemony in Iran was an already accomplished fact, according to many mullahs. Even the king and the queen were rumored to be new converts. Their "infamous sect," people said, promoted promiscuity and free sex, "Their religious meetings are a fornicating free-for-all." Their prophet was an impostor, a lecher, a pederast, and a foreign spy.

When a member of the Bahai faith introduced Pepsi and television to Iran, religious leaders immediately decreed Pepsi *najes* and television unsavory. The soft drink company was soon sold to more savory hands, and the government took over the television network. Yet, long after these transactions, the stigma continued to haunt Pepsi. The temptations of television, however, proved stronger than religious decrees.

In the innocence of my youth, I saw those assaults and insults as spontaneous but righteous responses of the pious people of Tehran. In the mid-seventies, through the casual boasting of a student, I first learned of an old, elaborate organization called the League to Combat

Bahaiism. It was (and so far as I know remains) a clandestine, hierarchical, organized, and well-funded organization that operates on several fronts. It discreetly propagates values and books inimical to the Bahai faith, and it infiltrates Bahai circles to learn the identity of its members and to gather information about their missionary plans. Bahais are famous for their missionary zeal, but to every place they sent a missionary, the League responded by dispatching their envoy. In the days after the Islamic Revolution, the League, often referred to as *Hojatiyeh*, became a major political force in Iran.

Of course many of the Bahais had by then seen the writing on the wall and had escaped before Islamic justice could catch up with them. Those that remained paid a heavy price. Some were killed by angry mobs. All known Bahais in the civil service were required to subject themselves to a degrading act of public recantation or lose their jobs and pensions. I knew a single mother of two teenage daughters who, after agonizing soul-searching, submitted to have her picture published in the newspaper in Islamic dress, with a note declaring her unflinching commitment to Islam and Shiism and her repugnance at the beguilings of that "infamous sect." I saw her wilt away with every passing day. Her two brothers refused to recant and the government appropriated the successful business they had built through long years of hard work. Defiant they remained, and I guess the camaraderie of their brethren helped them survive.

Finally there was the secular religion of my childhood. Idealizing history's inviolable laws and Stalin's infallible wisdom, it was called the Tudeh party, the party of the masses, and the fervor of its opponents was as strident as the faith of its followers.

I first encountered a party member when I was seven, on a visit to a distant relative. From overheard pieces of conversations, I had gathered that the son, Hossein, was a member. He had been arrested immediately after the coup of 1953 and spent about two years in prison. He had been only recently released.

He lived with his mother. He had a soft gentle face carved by the agonies of his defeat and incarceration, and a sadness in his eyes that was discernible even to my childhood sensibility. When my mother began her exhortations against the party and how it had led our youth to treason, heresy, and even espionage, Hossein, with a gesture more defiant than polite, suggested I take a walk with him up the stream that ran by the village of Evin.

It was a wonderful walk. It was the first time an adult

had talked to me as an equal, not as some one to be ordered, trained, and controlled. He spoke of nature, of its inexorable laws, of the beauty of silence. In his demeanor, and in the way he treated me, he provided an alternative model of "self-hood."

More and more morose and silent, Hossein spent the rest of his life with his mother. Over the years I heard about the physical abuse he had suffered in prison, about the anguish of witnessing the death of many of his friends, and of his vision of utopia. I once asked him why he had never married. "I am married to my past," he said, "and that's more than enough."

In later years I read about the Tudeh party's dismal record of internal dictatorship and external subservience to every whim of the Soviets. Remembering Hossein and other members of that party I had come to know, I had to wonder how such people, full of compassion and insight, could become commissars of a beastly totalitarian party and system. Maybe the greatest crime of the Tudeh party and other similar radical groups in Iran has not been their political opportunism or their quixotic obsession with ideological orthodoxy, but that they turned some of the most creative minds of the country into foot soldiers of totalitarianism.

—————— Covenant with the Colonel ——————

I first learned about it by accident, overhearing my mother talk to my father. "We have to fix his thing," my mother had said, and construing my father's silence as a sign of approval, added, "I'll have the colonel do it. He says he can come next week."

The colonel was my uncle. Lewd in his language and loose in his comportment, he was a rare, even rebellious, breed in the starchy atmosphere of our family. As children, we found his self-adulating tales of lechery, bribery, and extortion both funny and odd.

He arrived early that morning in his jeep. A sleepless night had numbed my fear. The night before, around bedtime, my mother, with studied casualness and an authority that nipped any gesture of resistance in the bud, officially informed me of the impending operation. "Everybody has to be circumcised," she said. She added that usually the operation is done earlier, but "in your case, we . . ." and here she hesitated, "sort of forgot. Your uncle will come tomorrow to take care of it. Don't worry. It's not a big deal."

By the time I was born, my mother had already conceived six times. I was the fourth to have survived. After her twelfth conception (and a fifth survivor), another uncle of mine, a surgeon by profession who was helping with the delivery, finally chose, on his own volition, to close my mother's fallopian tubes. "You aren't going to stop anyway," he told my father.

When the colonel finally arrived, my mother saw to my summary dispatch, pushing, in the last seconds, a neatly folded paisley bundle into my limp arms.

On the short drive to the hospital, my uncle appealed to my pending new identity. I was going to be a man, he said; and it would be an embarrassment to him if I "whined and whimpered like a little girl." His hat, worn in calculated hilarity more like a skull cap than the army uniform it was, and his words of reassurance were no solace.

Until a week before I, by then in the twelfth summer of my life, had not even known that I was different from other boys of my age. Curiosity about one's own body, let alone that of another, was strictly taboo. A few weeks before on a hot summer night as I was about to fall sleep, I suddenly heard my mother scream. The barrage, I soon realized, was directed at me. Perceiving a pernicious movement of my hands under the sheets, she had assumed—falsely I must add—that I was caressing myself. "Get your God-forsaken hands out of your *joon,*" she commanded. *Joon* in Persian is the vernacular form of *jan,* with a curious multiplicity of meanings. While in everyday language, it can refer to sexual organs, in philosophical discourse, it connotes the essence or soul of man. At the same time, it can simply mean life. *Joon* is also an expression of endearment when affixed to the end of a proper name. I find it curious that a society would make soul and essence coterminous with sexual organs yet impose forbidding strictures on any contact with those organs.

Thus estranged from my own *joon,* I had never seriously examined anybody else's genitals. Even at the public bath with my father and brothers we all followed extensive precautions so that others would not see our "thing" or we see theirs. And in the week preceding my operation, my friends who were then my only viable source of sexual enlightenment, would respond to my beleaguered inquiries with a tinge of malice and a heavy tone of sarcasm. "It's nothing. They just cut off half of your *dool*," they repeated.

The colonel parked his jeep in front of a two-story brick building surrounded by old weeping willows. A bronze plaque to the right of the entrance declared it to be Army Hospital Number One. It was, of course, no obstacle that I was not in the army or a dependent of a member of the armed forces. The hospital, as with all other governmental bureaucracies in Iran, served those who wielded power or connections, not their designated clients. In fact, government offices, invariably modeled after modern bureaucracies, were run more like feudal fiefdoms. Instead of becoming a catalyst for change, they were a source of inertia. Their meager but secure pay was sought after by everyone, and their power and services were monopolized by the few.

The colonel quickly dismounted and I followed glumly. I had to run to keep up with him, down a long corridor smelling of chloroform, up a few stairs, and we were there.

My chair of Elijah was an old operating table with chipped white enamel casings, and black leather cushions covered by a threadbare white sheet. A picture of the shah with a chest-full of royal insignias and the glossy eternal youth of the official photo etched on his face, hung on one of the walls. The colonel stood behind me, holding my hands and conversing with the operating doctor. The doctor wore white overalls, unkempt but adorned with the three stars of his rank. The two men were all but oblivious to my existence, let alone my mounting anxiety.

In the course of their casual chatter, my uncle, in his flippant manner, implored the doctor, "Don't cut too much. He'll need all you can spare him." Then out of compassion for what must have been my panicked pale face, he told me, "Don't worry; your *dool* will look better when Doc finishes with it." Interspersed with conversations about Kennedy, who had just been elected president and was pressuring the shah for reforms, and about real estate—for in those days land speculation had reached manic proportions in Tehran—my uncle went on to remind me how lucky I should feel.

"You know how they trimmed mine?" he asked. Knowing that nothing but a pained silence would be forthcoming, he told me. "The house was full of guests. I was about five. There was a knock on the door. Asghar walked in. I knew him. He had washed me several times in the public bath."

"Hold tight," the doctor interjected.

"The bastard was big. He carried a little bundle in his hand. I had heard that aside from washing, he bled you when you were sick and circumcised you when you were big."

The doctor amended the story, "Sometimes barbers did it."

"Then they grabbed me and took me to the room where the men were sitting. I saw him pull out his blade. My father began reciting Koranic verses. A couple of guys held my hands and feet. Yapping the name of *Hazrat-e Ali*, he cut half of my thing off and next thing I knew somebody from the next room, where the women and children had gathered, began to sing and play music. They covered me, waist down, with a red cloth and carried me back to the women's room."

Then pulling a long white baggy tunic out of the bundle my mother had sent along, my uncle told me to put on my new garb, and he spoke of the gifts he had received: nuts, a whistle, some cash, new moccasins, and a little monkey to keep as a pet.

The doctor told us of the small town he had come from, where circumcision used to be a major event. "Sometimes, if it was the son of a prominent family," he said, "the whole town would close down and celebrate.

The boy's family would give a feast."

I arrived home to a ready bed in an otherwise empty room. My brothers and sister were curious and kind. With the effects of local anesthesia gradually fading away, my pain increased sharply. Yet when my mother came home around noon and solemnly asked how I was, I could only respond that "my there stings." To elaborate about "there" with our parents would have been clearly outside the parameters of propriety. I could not tell her that shortly before her return, assisted by my sister, I had walked gingerly to the bathroom and, trying to urinate, had experienced the most excruciating pain of my life.

My father was even more distant. Shortly after his return from work, my mother briefed him on the successful operation, to which he only responded, "Thank God." While I have never doubted his love for me, and for all his children, I am still puzzled at the way he handled my trauma that day.

A few relatives who knew of my operation came to visit in the afternoon. With allusions that were meant to be both funny and polite, they talked of my belated circumcision. The few gifts I received were no match for the ordeal of that morning. If someone had told me that Abraham was circumcised when he was ninety-nine, I might have felt less chagrined.

A few days later, my uncle came again, this time unannounced. In his customary military language, full of profanities, he told me to come along and have my *dool* finally fixed.

At the hospital, the doctor lifted my tunic and told me to hold it. Then he yanked off half the bandages. Wincing, my uncle said, "Shh! Go easy on the animal." The rest of the bandages were removed and the wounds, upon examination, were decreed to be on their way to recovery.

Prometheus Bound

Four summers after my circumcision, I was on the plane to America. I remember the lights of the last Tehran dawn blurred through my tears. I knew it would be a long time before I would see them again. The agonies of saying farewell to the large contingent of family gathered at the airport had by then taken their toll. Numb, I sank into my seat, the sign indicating my tender age hung around my neck. I was to be delivered to my brother in California.

I sat near a kind American professor and his wife. He was returning home after a fellowship at Tehran University. Soon after takeoff, the stewardess handed me a small, rolled, steaming towel. When I saw others clean their hands and faces with it, I followed suit. There was something unforgettable and decadently sweet about the warmth and the aroma of that experience. When beverages were offered, I refused, and the professor, guessing the reason for my refusal, used his little Persian and my meager English to inform me that soft drinks were free.

The food was even more problematic. All my life, I have been a timid eater, reluctant to experiment with unknown or exotic dishes. On that flight, every dish seemed dangerously exotic. I nibbled at the food, picking at safe corners. When we landed in London, I was hungry enough to eat an English deviled egg sandwich, and thus it was that I was introduced to white bread, that culinary wonder of the West.

I was worn out by the time I arrived in San Francisco. With short stops in Athens and London, the trip had taken nearly thirty hours. My brother and two of his friends were waiting at the airport. Rejoicing at the sight, I jumped to kiss my sibling. With a gentle shove of the elbow, he nudged me away and said, "In America, men don't kiss one another." In Iran, the sight of young men holding hands, or of men of any age kissing one another's cheeks in public was, and is, a perfectly acceptable sight— a token of Platonic love.

On the road home from the airport, nothing seemed ordinary. The freeways with six lanes, the Bay Bridge, the skyscrapers, the beauty of the bay all had a dreamlike luminosity. Not even my exhaustion could dampen the feeling of joy and amazement.

In those days, my brother worked for an interior decorator. "Room and board, plus a little cash is what I get," he said. The decorator had been kind enough to say I could stay with them for a while.

It was about nine in the evening when we finally arrived at the house. When we entered the spacious living room, Robert, the decorator, was lying on a couch. Another man, whose name I soon learned to be Jerry, was sitting nearby on the carpet. Even to my virgin eyes, the angle of his repose had unmistakable meaning. I had heard of pederasty. Men in love with other men was a novelty.

I was introduced to Robert and Jerry. Neither man rose to greet me. A brisk motion of the hands and a curt "Hi" was all I received. Though I had heard of the casual ways of Americans, the behavior of the two men still seemed strange.

I spent the night in one of three guest rooms. In the morning Hassan, hiding his anger behind an unconvincing casualness said, "We have to find you a place today."

I agreed. Early that morning, I had overheard his conversation with Robert. Even my paltry English was enough to understand its gist. I was supposed to have slept in my brother's room. The guest room was for guests and I was now one of the help. My exhilaration at having arrived in America was momentarily eclipsed by a debilitating sense of humiliation.

By the end of that day, I had a room of my own. An American friend of my brother agreed to take me in as a roommate. Like Hassan, he was an engineering student. He worked as a truck driver for three months in the summer and went to school the rest of the year. We lived on the margin of poverty. Spam was his main diet, mine was hard-boiled eggs. We rented two rooms, a small kitchen, and a bath from Mrs. Goats.

She was an old lady of about eighty. Deeply wrinkled and fiercely independent, she clumped around the house in a clearly audible limp. Her son visited her once a month. The loneliness of her life seemed reprehensible to me. I blamed the son. I remembered the reverence we all had for my grandmother. Her six sons and her daughter visited her every day. Each time her grandchildren saw her, we were expected to kiss her hands. The loneliness of Mrs. Goats' life made even our ritualized gestures of love for my grandmother seem the height of devotion.

By the end of my first week in America, I had a job delivering newspapers. In the shack where the paperboys gathered to pick up their bundles, I was the oldest. Our route leader was a man of about twenty with the kind of perpetual adolescence that one often finds in Boy Scout leaders.

It was summer then. I had no friends. When school began, I gradually realized that high school students were considered too old to be delivering papers. Hiding my job from my new friends became a serious problem and a perpetual concern.

To make ends meet, I also took on odd jobs, watering lawns for a nursing home, cutting the grass for neighbors. The job at the nursing home was my favorite. My supervisor there was a jolly old Irish man who took particular pride in his garden. It took me a few months to prove to him that I was worthy and capable of watering his flower beds and the front lawn. Until then I was only permitted to work in the orchard and the less visible parts of the yard. The old ladies at the nursing home were also very kind to me. They had heard that I lived away from my family and usually went out of their way to make me feel accepted. Rarely a week passed when at least one of the ladies did not have some little gift for me—an old comic book, an Easter egg, a little metal frame emptied of its old picture. The other advantage of the nursing home was that I ate my best meal of the week there. Occasionally I even worked for Robert, the decorator. For a while my job was to buy books. But this was no easy matter. My orders were to purchase books of the same size and same binding color. "We need six feet of maroon," he once told me. He was decorating a hair salon.

It was a hot summer day, three weeks since I had moved into my new flat. The Beatles were on their way to San Francisco. The elation of living on my own was only occasionally clouded by the anxieties of charting unknown waters.

Bored with my incessant English lessons, some of which included listening to Barry Goldwater on the stump, I went to play some tennis. I had just bought a cheap racket. Before the summer was out, it curled under the heat. As I clumsily practiced against the wall, a girl about my age arrived at the court and began playing a few steps away from me. Guardedly, I watched her from the corner of my eye.

After a few tense moments, she came over and asked, "You want to play?"

"I'm no good," I replied.

"Neither am I."

We played until the heat got the better of us. In the

shade of a tree, we sat on a bench and talked about our
lives, about my attempt to learn English, about the land
I had come from. She had never heard of Iran. Like many
Americans in those days, she confused it with Iraq.
Ironically, it was years later that Ayatollah Khomeini and
his escapades finally ended that confusion. My tennis
partner was less interested in geography and more
impressed with the fact that I lived in my own apartment.
She wanted to see my flat.

My room was furnished with a single bed, a large
wooden desk, and a creaky old chair. The walls were barren. She sat on the bed. I brought two large glasses of iced
lemonade and before I could sit on the chair, she patted
the mattress beside her and with a disarming casualness
said, "Why not here, it's more comfortable."

I was all ears. I wanted to understand every word. After
all, this was a new language I was learning. I desired not
to miss any of the mysteries intuitively understood by men
and women all over the world. But even erotic intuition
can be stymied by cultural differences. Societies often have
their own peculiar semiotics of erotic love and, what little
I knew of sex was Iranian in origin. My new puberty added
to my awkward combination of zeal and timidity.

Nothing in my limited carnal knowledge had prepared

me for what was to come. All the kisses with my cousin had been hurried and hidden, more a gesture than a consummated act. But now consummation was at hand. The feel of this girl's lips and tongue was at once luscious and lurid. I was beset by sensual and emotional dissonance; craving consummation, I was also repulsed by what in my vocabulary of those days could only be called lascivious lust. I was livid and aroused and mortified. Every cell was a volcano, with the lava of youth seething to erupt. And when the eruption came, it delivered as much confusion as comfort.

Even at the height of my confusion, I knew I was luckier than most of my Iranian peers, whose first carnal knowledge was gained in the seamy cubicles of a whorehouse with a curtain separating them from other customers and their inhospitable partners. I used to hear my schoolmates recount the tales of their secret sojourns to those infamous houses—called, ironically, "the New City." The rest of us listened, our prurient curiosities aroused. Now I had experienced sex in my own bed with an eager partner of my own age, and yet I was confused. After that day, I saw little of her. We attended the same school, but I often tried to avoid her.

Oakland Tech was what we called our school, short for Oakland Technical High School. It was predominantly

black. It is only in retrospect that this seems somehow
significant. Racism was not a part of my emotional vocabulary in those days. The bigotry and rancor I had been
raised with was not racial, but ethnic and religious. Our
school was amicably peaceful. Today, students of Oakland
Tech go through metal detectors to enter the buildings
that we once so casually sauntered through.

Though I had entered Oakland Tech as a tenth grader,
I finished high school in one year. I received credits for
knowing French, and the fact that Iranian high schools
emulated the old German and French models and were
academically far more demanding than American schools
facilitated my early exit. I was seventeen when I entered
Merritt, a community college in the heart of West
Oakland's black neighborhood. Today, the school has
moved to an affluent hillside that is predominantly white.
The beautiful old Arabesque buildings that once housed
Merritt College stand derelict. High fences and boarded
windows guard it against homeless squatters.

Bobby Seale and Huey Newton gave me my first taste
of radicalism. Until then, *The Catcher in the Rye* was my
closest brush with rebellion. I read Mark's copy late in my
high school year. He was our school's one and only beat-
nik. I visited his house often; the place was usually messy

and always cluttered with books. His family had a monkey for pet. Everything about their house was exotic and different from the starchy atmosphere of my childhood home. Yet, it was with Mark and his parents that I felt most at ease.

But Bobby Seale was no Holden Caulfield. Often, he stormed the cafeteria during lunch hours and declaimed his radical message of black power and violence to an awed and subdued audience. One such day, as I listened intently to Seale's angry sermon, a woman I had noticed before came and sat by me. I had admired her from afar for at least three weeks, amazed and engrossed by her beauty, yet too timid to start a conversation. I worried that she had come to chastise me for my staring. When she began to talk, her soft voice and graceful demeanor calmed all my anxieties. And thus it was that I first fell in love in America. The more time I spent with her, the more the image of my cousin, the love of my younger years, faded. Through Caroline, an African-American woman, I learned about the sounds of Myriam Makeba and the poetry of Claude McKay. It was with her that I first learned the ecstasies of an erotic encounter when touched by the power of love.

After two years we parted when I went on to the

University of California at Berkeley. It was 1968, and
Mario Savio and the Free Speech Movement were
already history, and I was becoming involved in a burgeoning movement of Iranian students fighting the Shah.

The growth of a large movement of opposition among
Iranian students was, I think, an interesting historical
paradox. The Pahlavi regime, bent on modernizing Iran,
needed technocrats. They sent thousands of students
abroad for training; all but a small minority ended up in
the West. In those days, the Iranian regime saw Marxism
as its main enemy. Democratic societies of Europe and
America were considered safe.

The mistake of the Pahlavis is reminiscent of the tragic
error of the Romanovs in Russia and of the Israeli authorities in the Occupied Territories. Fearful of the growth of
democratic ideals in nineteenth century Russia, tsars sent
their students to Prussia instead of France and England,
and it was in autocratic Prussia that Russians learned their
first lesson in Marxism. In our own times, in the mid-
eighties, Israeli authorities favored the growth of religious
forces in the Occupied Territories as an antidote to the
radicalism of the PLO. In none of these cases did things
work out as planned.

In the case of Iran, the regime's plans backfired in two

ways. The democratic aspirations of the newly educated technocrats became a major force in overthrowing the monarchy; and in the sixties, while the Marxist Soviet Union smothered under totalitarianism, it was the West that caught the contagious fever of revolution and Marxist theory. Many of us, disgruntled as we were with the political realities of Iran, were also consumed by that fever.

For us, inspiration came not from Woodstock but from the dour example of Mao's Cultural Revolution. While the flower children made their pilgrimages to Haight-Ashbury and Telegraph Avenue in Berkeley in search of higher and higher levels of psychedelic consciousness, my comrades and I congregated every Wednesday in a little bookstore called Yenan, where pictures of Mao, Stalin, Lenin, and Marx adorned the walls. An always-jovial American ran the store. Wednesday was when the weekly English edition of the Peking Review arrived. While in retrospect almost everything about the journal seems embarrassingly banal, in those days we read it with relish and saw it as our gateway to higher and higher levels of political consciousness.

Like the Gnostics of the past, we cherished our secret cult and saw ourselves as exiles in the world, responsible for lighting the way to salvation. Iranian history is replete with tales of clandestine Gnostic cults committed to enlightening the befuddled masses. All profess to some secret knowledge about the sacred riddle of life. In our turn, history was the riddler and we were its infallible interpreters. We spent endless hours and countless days in abstract and obtuse debates about this riddle. Once, three of us were chosen to see how Mao's theories about what he had called "semi-feudal, semi-colonial" societies applied to Iran. My partners were a woman about whom I knew nothing at the time and an eccentric friend I had known for three years.

We three rented a house in the ghettoes of Oakland for reasons more ideological than economical. We wanted to be close to the "oppressed masses." For nearly two years, we worked at this study long hours every day. We pored over economic statistics, monographs, and books. We read and reread Mao's handful of essays on economics.

We concluded that Mao's theory lacked sufficient clarity. But, of course, we dared not say that in such stark terms. Instead, in our final report, we wrote that we three lacked a sufficient grasp of both Mao's thoughts and the reality of Iranian society. The problem, in other words, wasn't with Mao, but with our own insufficient revolutionary fervor.

Soon after, our group dispersed. I never saw my eccentric friend again. He returned to Iran, and within five years, was executed by the Islamic Republic. The woman was luckier. She fled Iran on foot. She now lives in Paris, pursues a career as a painter, and disdains all politics.

Today, the efforts of our research team seem to me futile and full of quixotic illusions of grandeur, but I cannot remember another project to which I more fully applied myself, or from which I derived a greater sense of self-importance and satisfaction. Those abstract theoretical debates had a narcotic quality. The more we indulged in them, the less we had the ability to rid ourselves of their lure. Furthermore, by rejecting any who belittled our theoretical obsessions, we confirmed our image of ourselves as a righteous yet persecuted elite.

It was on the night of the moon landing, I was a part-time bartender in a Berkeley restaurant. Though everyone had been clamoring to get that historic night off, I had volunteered to work. Swimming against the tide, Mao had said, was a good thing. Other activists of the Iranian student movement, I later heard, had also met that night and after a brief discussion decided not to watch the moon landing on television. "It is part of an imperialist design to militarize space," they had concurred. As a human feat, the landing had at the time no significance for us. Politics and class struggle was the only prism through which we saw and analyzed the world.

Our indifference to the moon landing was also tinged by our anti-Americanism born partly out of the political climate of the sixties, and the close ties between the U.S. government and the Shah of Iran. Of equal relevance, I think, is what Orwell called "negative nationalism." Fearful as we were of being consumed or assimilated into the new American culture, our anti-Americanism was at least partially our way of clinging to some semblance of national identity and inuring ourselves against the temptations of the West. No wonder then that in spite of our near neurotic disparagement of nationalism as a bourgeois disease, we invariably called our meeting places "Iran House." Even in the euphoria of the sixties, the craving for home, the nostalgia for Iran, was a force more galvanizing than all of our politically correct internationalist slogans.

In fact, the lure of community was our greatest offering to potential recruits. Finding new members, or what we patronizingly called "the young masses," was our constant preoccupation. Rival organizations each had their own strategies for recruiting, and fought fiercely for the privilege to court a newcomer.

I recruited a girl to our group who had been the child-hood friend of my future wife. I met her at the airport when she arrived in the United States. By then I already knew a great deal about her. By the end of the first week, I had spun a protective web around her. I had usurped the role of her personal manager. In everything from finding a room to landing a job, I was there to help, and for a newcomer to a strange land, few things are as appreciated as the assistance of a compatriot. But I had an ulterior motive, and my conversation gradually moved from casual complaints about hard times in Iran to militant propositions about the need to fight dictatorship. She only learned of my original intent when she was more than a willing convert to our cause.

It was more than simple community and nostalgia that attracted us to Iran House. For some, radicalism was a gesture toward immortality. "Revolution," "the cause," and "the oppressed" were transcendental phenomena we could cling to. For others, it was a gesture toward justice. Some of us felt guilty about our affluent parents; others were possessed of egalitarian passion. We were all infat-uated with a cult of poverty and tantalized by proletarian life. We feigned poverty and sought material deprivation.

I remember a political conference I attended. A dozen of us stayed with a friend named Abbas, the son of one of Iran's wealthiest families. He lived in a one-bedroom apartment in the Oakland ghettoes. A picture of Mao, with that perennially gleeful smile on his face, was the only decoration on the walls. There was a couch and a bed in the apartment. As a gesture of poverty that night, we all slept on the floor. "The proletariat has no beds," I remember someone saying. Two decades later I learned, not without bitterness, that in those very years, Mao, our paragon of proletarian virtues, slept in the opulent beds of past emperors in the Forbidden City and often had young girls share the bed with him.

Abbas returned to Iran on the eve of the Revolution. He reclaimed his share of his family's fortune and donated nearly all of it to the cause. He died in a gun battle with Islamic Revolutionary Guards. While for thousands, student radicalism had been a fling, a romantic gesture, for Abbas it was a passion, a lifelong commitment to justice. His fate, similar to scores of other activists of those days, remains a reminder of the high cost our generation of Iranians have paid for the temptations of our youth.

At the same time, our radicalism was a gesture toward debunking patriarchy. It was a defiance both literal and metaphoric. The king was, after all, called "The Crowned Father." But like all metaphoric resolutions of historic problems, this one had its genealogy in individual needs and problems. I think my radicalism was at least partially a crutch I used to stand up to my patriarchal past. I gained strength that it was not just "I," but an amorphous, communal, historical "we" that rebelled against him and all he had become a symbol of.

Politics was for us also a mission and when politics becomes a mission it often assumes a dangerously self-referential morality in which the ends justify any devious means. To us the world and all its inhabitants were instruments to be used in our war. I encouraged the girl I had recruited into our group to steal the passport of a friend who had traveled two thousand miles to visit her. The reckless ethics of revolution sometimes legitimizes our demons. It was infused with such a reckless spirit that three weeks after submitting my dissertation, I returned to Iran.

─────────────────── El Dorado ───────────────────

Tehran had only a makeshift airport when I landed there in 1975. A few weeks before, a heavy snowstorm had caused the collapse of the roof at the main terminal.

In my childhood the airport wasn't just a port of travel; it was a novelty, a mysterious attraction, a gateway of wonderment. To eat in its restaurant had been the ultimate culinary experience. Now the building was a ruin.

Rumors connected the collapse of the building to the corruption of officials. The contractor had been the infamous "Mr. Five Percent," so called because he was said to receive that much commission on every government contract. He was the president of the Senate, a close confidante of the shah, and partners with some members of the royal family. Relying on these connections, and reaping windfall profits, he had ignored certain engineering specifications in the construction of the airport terminal. An unusually heavy blizzard that winter was more than the flimsy building could bear. But that night, as my plane landed, I had other things to worry about.

Our plane stopped somewhere in the middle of the tarmac. There was snow on the ground. A bus took us to the entrance of a large tent. The interior was Spartan, its only adornment a grotesquely huge black and white photograph of the shah, ornately framed, looming from one of the upright tent poles. The shah wore a handsome civilian suit, the stern smile of royalty, his right hand frozen between an act of benediction and a Nazi salute. In spite of his modern dress, he looked like a prophet descending from heaven. Clouds were his firmament. Underneath the picture, sewn to the tent, were the words, "God, King, Country. " Under his picture, I handed my passport to the young officer at one of three control booths in the tent.

He offered a routine welcome and began nonchalantly to browse through a list in front of him. The dreaded list, I had heard, consisted of two categories of dissidents: those whose passports were impounded upon entry and were asked to report to the police at some later time, and those who were arrested on the spot. Frightened by the prospect that my name might be on the list, I had not told my family the time of my arrival. For the same precautionary reasons, Fereshteh, the woman with whom I was returning to Iran, the woman whom I was soon to marry, stood in a different line, a little further back.

Political crimes were, in those days, contagious. When an offender was arrested those with him were also taken in—"just in case they too are guilty" is how the arresting officer explained it to me a couple of years later. Thus, had my name been on the dreaded enemies list, my separation from Fereshteh would have spared her the danger of arrest and allowed her to inform my family of my fate.

"It's cold in here," I said to the officer, hoping to hide behind idle chatter the agonies of those few long seconds of waiting. By then he had already begun to stamp my passport. As he handed it to me, he said, "It's temporary. They'll build another one soon." With studied calm, I took my passport, picked up my luggage, and went into a city I hardly knew.

It was near midnight when, after dropping Fereshteh at her mother's, I rang the bell to my parents' house. The home of my childhood was long gone. I had not seen my father for eleven years. He was an old man when he opened the door. We embraced silently, and we wept; a short recompense for long years of separation. His first words were to my mother. "Madam, your son has arrived."

Much of the next day and some of the next week was spent visiting family and friends. Early in the afternoon of my first full day in Tehran, I hit the streets. The neighborhood of my childhood, my old school, new buildings, old faces were all fascinating to me. It was on that walk, I think, that better than ever I realized what it means to live in your own land. Having experienced the transience of living as a foreigner in a different country, having known the vacuity of avenues and houses that conjure no memory, I cherished the permanence of home. Nothing about the contours of the city, about the sounds and smells of streets, seemed insignificant that day. I felt I was where I belonged.

About five weeks after that walk, Fereshteh and I were married. Though the ceremonies were simple, the circumstances leading to the event were neither simple nor pleasant. My family was unequivocally opposed to the marriage. In fact, on the first night of my arrival in Tehran, after about half an hour of pleasantries and family gossip, my mother told me about the young daughter of a prominent family she had recently visited, and about the family's desire to meet me as soon as possible. Then, in passing, as if confirming a foregone conclusion, she said, "And about that girl, I want you to know that marrying her is simply out of question."

"The issue is not even open for discussion," I responded, hoping to end the unexpected turn in the conversation and avoid acrimony on my first night in Tehran.

I knew my family had heard about Fereshteh. They knew she and I had lived together in Berkeley for three years, and that fact alone, in their mind, disqualified her as a suitable bride. They had a litany of other complaints as well. They wanted me to marry a rich, young, innocent girl of their choice.

A month after that aborted discussion, one day, around lunch time, I ambushed my parents with the news of my impending marriage.

"I've decided to marry Fereshteh," I said nervously, "and I wanted to inform you, and hopefully receive your blessings."

My mother spoke first, and with the kind of candor that was one of her hallmarks, said, "You will do no such thing and you certainly do not have our permission."

"I was not asking for permission," I responded. And before I had a chance to deliver the long sermon I had prepared, the cordial conversation turned into a barrage of threats and admonishments. "I will disinherit you," my father said, and my mother warned that God's most fearsome wrath is reserved for those who defy their mother's desires. In spite of the vehemence of their pronouncements, Fereshteh and I were married the next day.

Ours was a marriage of love. In fact, I had fallen in love with her long before I had met her. In retrospect, it seems to me that I was in love not with her, but with the idea of her, and I remember the moment when that love began.

One night, as I was working as a bartender in Berkeley, my dear friend, Ardy, came to visit. After a while, he began to read me a short story his sister had written. I had heard about that sister, about her keen mind and her fine prose. I was deeply moved by the story. When a few months later she arrived in the Bay Area, she was even more impressive than I had imagined. She could recite Hafez and converse knowledgeably about Camus and Castro. She quoted Simon de Beauvoir and swept me off my feet. She was a perfect catalyst for my nascent Romantic attachments to both Iran and to the idea of revolution. From the very first day I met her, our relationship was filled with both love and tension. Love, I believed, would be the elixir of all of our problems, and so it was that I decided to defy my parents and marry Fereshteh.

Commensurate with our radical ethos of the day, we chose to forego a large wedding ceremony and instead simply went to the office of the notary public, where according to Iranian law, all marriages and divorces had to be registered.

An appointment was made for eight o'clock at night. By the time I arrived Fereshteh and her family were already there. My two brothers, the only siblings then living in Iran, were also expected but I soon learned that my mother, upon hearing of my plans, had forbidden my brothers to attend the ceremonies. Maybe it was callous of me to put my brothers in the position where they had to choose between me and my mother, but that night I was both hurt and disconsolate. Hassan, my guardian angel when I first arrived in America, was to have been my witness. Throughout my adult life, his kindness to me has known no bounds. Yet, that night, in deference to my mother, he chose not to appear at the ceremony, forcing me to scrounge for a witness at the last minute. The mullah who was supposed to perform the ceremonies threatened to close shop if I was not back with a viable attendant in less than fifteen minutes.

The relative or friend living closest to the mullah's office was Fereshteh's uncle. I hurried to his house, knocked at the door, and to my great dismay found him absolutely drunk. He invited me in. He was a gentle man, cruel to himself, kind to others, and addicted to the formalities of life. Refusing his invitation to go in was simply not an option. When he learned the purpose of my visit, he tried to convince me that he was fit to serve, but I knew the mullah would have a fit if I returned with a drunken witness. With as much finesse as I could muster, I finally excused myself and set out to look for someone else.

As I was about to leave the apartment building, I ran into a friend I had met at Berkeley and not seen for several years. After perfunctory greetings, I asked, "Are you free for the next fifteen minutes?"

"Why?" he said with surprise.

"Can you be a witness at my wedding?" Judging by the expression on his face, he was not exactly honored at my invitation but agreed to come along anyway. A few minutes later, I was a married man.

After the ceremony, my witness left to go home and Fereshteh's family and I went to celebrate the occasion with a small dinner party at a restaurant. But by then, the anxieties of the last forty-eight hours had begun to take their toll. Before long, I was sick enough to be rushed to the emergency room. I spent the first night of my married life in a hospital.

By the time of my marriage, I already had a job. It had taken me all of ten minutes to be hired as an assistant professor of political science at the National University of Iran. In those days, professors were in high demand. Whereas in the early forties there had been one university in Iran, by the mid-seventies there were close to 150 active institutions of higher learning in the country. Italian, French, and Austrian diploma mills, where a "doctorate" could be purchased with less than a year of college, had helped saturate the mushrooming Iranian academia with many sham doctors. All the Dean of the School of Economics and Political Science needed to hear was that I had an American Ph.D.

"Can you begin to work in two weeks?" he asked. He added that classes began in one week, "But it'll take at least two weeks for the thing." I feigned ignorance.

"What thing?"

"You know, they have to give you a clearance. It usually takes several months. But I know somebody there. Nobody can start teaching without it."

Languages find curious ways to reflect, and deflect, political realities. Those days in Iran, SAVAK was a central fixture of politics. Yet public discourse was all but devoid of any direct reference to that organization. Like Satan, whose very name was feared and avoided by medieval man, the word "SAVAK" was almost never spoken aloud. "It," "they," or "the thing" were used in the vernacular to refer to the actions of an organization that had, by the mid-seventies, permeated every facet of life in Iran.

After three weeks of anxious waiting, "the thing" finally came. The relative expedience of "its" arrival gave me a sense of comfort. I surmised that SAVAK knew little of my anti-government activities abroad, and with the arrival of the coveted security clearance, I began to teach.

But teaching in Iran was different than I had imagined. In social sciences, there were almost no texts available. In nearly all classes, readings were limited to mimeographed notes prepared by professors. In some cases, teachers spent the whole class time dictating comically out-of-date notes. While in private, students sometimes ridiculed such clumsy teachers, few dared challenge them openly. Many topics were strictly taboo, others were highly sensitive. Marx was not mentioned, except in cursory criticism. Too much criticism of royalty, even that of distant times and lands, was suspect. Needless to say, political issues relating to the internal politics of contemporary Iran were altogether off limits.

Each class was assumed to have at least one agent of the secret police. If sensitive topics had to be broached, then elaborate metaphors, naively believed to be incomprehensible to the SAVAK, were used. For instance, instead of directly referring to Marxism, we talked of the "scientific world view." Students craved any reference to taboo topics. Professors who dared tread such treacherous waters became instant academic celebrities. For me in those days, part of the spiritual meaning of teaching was derived from mastering this subterranean political language and escaping detection. I felt part of a secret brotherhood. We courted danger. Teaching had become a mission, a game of intellectual stealth for the right to preach to the convert.

Though in retrospect the game seems absurdly romantic, in those days it infused my life, and I guess the lives of many like me, with a deep sense of significance. A kind of asceticism, suffering, and even martyrdom had become part of the spirituality of our intellectual life. Influenced as we were by the Russian notion of the intelligentsia, we had become a secular version of the warrior-knight messiah who has always been an imminent part of our society's eschatology. If in years past, the twelfth Imam, now absent for more than a millennium, was expected to come and single-handedly actualize the promised millennia, in our days, we took that role for ourselves. It was in further search of such a role that finally, a few weeks after settling into my job at the university, I contacted Hamid.

I met him at a designated bus stop, and I was afraid. On two earlier occasions, after elaborate precautionary measures, a meeting with him had been arranged, and on both occasions, I had failed to show up. Each time, I lied and said that I had misunderstood the time or the place of our meeting. The truth was that I knew meeting him would commence a new and dangerous chapter in my life, and I was hesitant. But fervor eventually overcame my hesitation and a new meeting was scheduled. A rolled sports magazine in my left hand, the day's newspaper under his right arm, a question about the destination of the bus, and an almost absurd response about it going "somewhere near the center of the city," and we met.

"Call me Hamid," he said. I knew almost nothing about him, save that he had entered Iran covertly, lived underground, and was fighting against the regime. It was only several years later, after his death, that I learned more. Police claimed he was killed in an armed battle with security forces. Dissidents claimed he was arrested and tortured to death. For me, the fact of his death made the manner of his dying less significant.

His real name was Vaez-zadeh. He had been at the top of his class in high school and had gone to Italy to become an architect. He had shown much talent and had won a government scholarship. A year before graduation, he gave it all up, traveled on forged documents to Communist China and after a six-month course in revolutionary theory and practice, joined the Kurdish rebels in Iran. When I met him, he had been in the country for about six years.

There is, in literature, particularly in Russian novels of the nineteenth century, an ideal romantic image of a revolutionary. He is young, jovial but earnest in disposition, a paragon of humility and compassion, unbending in principles, obsessive in scruples, single minded in purpose, and fearless. Hamid was as close to this ideal as I have ever seen.

We met regularly, never for longer than a couple of hours. We walked in crowded streets as we talked. "Camouflage is the key," Hamid would often say. We exchanged what news we had, exaggerating any indications of struggle against the regime and belittling all ominous portents. Delusive as these tactics seem today, in those days they were the only tonic strong enough to keep us committed to our otherwise desperately hopeless and dangerous task. Intractable utopianism convinced us that such meetings were the germs of the future revolution, and the regime's incurable paranoia convinced them of the same. Patrols roamed the city in search of peripatetic revolutionaries. Suspicious pedestrian pairs were suddenly stopped, separated, and interrogated about the nature of their conversation. If the two accounts seemed incompatible, the pair would be arrested. In anticipation, Hamid and I had rehearsed a whole dialogue to recount. In the end, all the precautions were for nothing. Hamid's closest comrade had been a mole all along.

Fear was, of course, not the only characteristic of the old monarchy's schizoid relationship with the intellectuals. I know of no other contemporary regime that was as awed and enamored of intellectuals as the Pahlavi regime. The government wooed them desperately, yearned for their political approval, and paid handsomely for their allegiance.

A few months after my arrival at the university, a colleague who was known to be a political operative of the regime, and soon became a powerful minister, invited me to tea. He talked of a "think tank" connected to the queen, of the freedom of criticism in the group, of the queen's desire to become a force for reform, and of "my responsibility" to contribute to the process.

"Why me?" I asked.

"The students seem to like you."

I refused politely, but he persisted. I promised to think about it. I consulted Hamid, and he urged me to join. "How can you refuse?" he said. "It's an invitation into the belly of the beast."

I joined the think tank with great reluctance. It was a small group of educated technocrats committed to both their own private gain and to a tentative and ambiguous agenda for modernization. Essentially, the group studied social problems and tried to offer solutions. At the same time, it was a crucible for elite recruitment. For many, it became a springboard to powerful political positions. A few participants, including myself, were also occasionally used as ghostwriters for the queen.

One day, after having prepared one such royal speech, I was sitting in the office of the minister who headed the group. The phone rang, he answered and then leaped to his feet, stood at attention, and offered his oral supplications to the queen. There was more than sheer comedy in the spectacle. The call was about a word in the prepared speech with which the queen was unfamiliar.

It was through participation in that group that I learned

about the fractured nature of power in Iran. Behind the facade of a monolithic monarchy were fiercely contentious factions. There was a group connected to the shah's sister, another loyal to the prime minister and a third group attached to the powerful minister of court, Alam. I saw that old guard politicians despised the new technocrats; I even heard about a fierce struggle between Anglophile politicians and some who were thought to be close to the American government.

Most incredible of all, I saw that the vast majority of the technocrats who worked for the old regime were apologetic for it, and in private articulated dismay with and disdain for the government.

For all their courting of the intellectuals, in a fundamental sense, the Pahlavi regime lacked legitimacy amongst most of them. At the core of the political discourse was an insuperable rift between a perennially guilty "they," and a perpetually innocent and oppressed "we." "They" were blamed for all social ills. We even denied or denigrated their obvious accomplishments.

I remember a tour I went on with thirty students, in my first spring as a teacher in Iran. The university had paid for the trip. Its purpose was an education in society's rapid development. About half the students were of leftist persuasion, the other half were devout Muslims. All were openly against the regime. Their camaraderie in fighting a common foe overcame the waves of ideological tensions that passed between them.

The Revolution has destroyed the amity we all felt on that trip. Several of the Islamic students went on to become powerful figures in the Islamic Republic. I know that at least five of the leftist students have since been shot by the Islamic regime's firing squads.

Our tour took us to Sistan and Baluchistan, one of the poorest corners of Iran, near the Pakistani border. It had once been the land of Rostam, the hero of the *Shahnameh*, Iran's grand epic. Other histories describe its lush forests and valiant people. Now, only the old still lived there, the young having long since left for the city. Encroaching desert haunted many now-derelict villages, while in the cities, amidst the squalor of mud huts, we often saw new empty brick buildings.

They had been built to house much-needed health facilities. But after constructing the buildings, and amassing impressive statistics on the number of new health clinics, the government realized that there weren't enough doctors to operate the facilities. Few Iranian physicians would accept the emotional challenge and the financial constraints that went with serving in such remote areas. In desperation, the government began to import doctors.

In one village, an old man told us about an Indian doctor who had worked at the clinic for about a month.

"The doctor spoke no Persian," the old villager said.

"How did you tell him where the pain was?" I asked.

"By signs. Pain is easy to show."

Finally, after a young girl died of diarrhea, the doctor was driven out by the villagers. "He didn't know much," the old man said.

In the land of such villages a four-lane modern highway was under construction. Confused by the anomaly of the sight, and anchored to an ideology in which the shah's regime was incapable of doing anything positive for the country, the student sitting next to me on the bus asked, "We keep saying this regime is reactionary and can't do any good for the people. What about this highway?"

I knew the answer all too well. I told him about the nature of politically dependent regimes like the shah's and that they were incapable of truly modernizing their societies. I explained the road's military use. "It is to connect the military base at the tip of the Persian Gulf to the Soviet borders. Americans wanted it built."

We even managed to turn into tools of subversion the

funds provided by the university to cover our trip. The
university had not only chartered a bus for us, but paid
me the equivalent of one month's salary as a bonus for
spending my new year holiday on the tour, and also provided me with a generous discretionary fund for feeding
and housing my students.

On the first day of the trip, I informed the students that
I was not going to take the bonus for myself, and that if
any money was left over from the discretionary fund at
the end of the trip, that money and my bonus could be
used for any purpose the students voted for.

For this reason, and also because of our belief in the
virtues of an ascetic life, every night we lodged for free in
classrooms in different schools. We each had a pair of
blankets or a sleeping bag. Canned beans and bread were
the major staples of our diet. When the tour ended, a
large sum of money was left over. The students decided
that the money should be discreetly turned over to the
two student libraries in our department. In those days,
nearly all departments at the university had at least two
such libraries, one run by leftist, the other by Islamic students. The rooms were both gathering places for activists
against the regime. So instead of educating us about the
developments in Iran, the tour only strengthened our

resolve and increased our resources for fighting the regime. Aside from distorted dictates of ideology, there were, I think, historical as well as political roots to our generation's distrust of the modernizing intentions of the Pahlavi regime.

Monarchies ultimately derive at least part of their legitimacy from a form of divine right, and all divine rights need a sufficiently ambiguous and opaque beginning around which a myth of divine origin can be woven. But the genesis of the Pahlavi dynasty, and the undeniable role of foreign powers in bringing Reza Shah, founder of the dynasty, to power, were too transparent to beget or sustain a claim of divine right. And if dubious genealogy undermined the father's claim to divine rights, the 1953 coup permanently tarnished the son's political legitimacy. In that year, after more than a decade of tumultuous rule, the shah, frustrated by a burgeoning democratic and nationalist movement, fled the country. Soon, he was returned to power by a military coup. It was an open secret in Iran, and in the West, that the coup was masterminded by British and American intelligence services.

As a result of the coup, the opposition with its nucleus of intellectuals lost a political battle but won moral and cultural supremacy. Henceforth, any cooperation with the

regime became synonymous with betrayal. The few intellectuals of the opposition who, over the years, chose to
work with the regime, were invariably forced to perform
degrading rituals of public repentance, losing all their
credibility in the process. In a sense, the old regime's relationship to these intellectuals was necrophilic; it destroyed
and devitalized what it desired to possess.

For me, Parviz Nik-khah epitomized this necrophilia.
A handsome, articulate man of great valor, he had become
the hero of the opposition when, in the mid-sixties, during his trial on charges of conspiracy to commit regicide,
he took the offensive and attacked the regime for its corruption and social incompetence. "History shall absolve
me," he told the military tribunal.

He had served four years of a five-year sentence when he
suddenly experienced a political change of mind. The opposition had been wrong, he said. It must join forces with the
Pahlavi regime and expedite Iran's march to modernity.

Some said he was tortured; others claimed a new drug
had been used to induce new ideas in him. Many thought
he had made a deal with the devil. Few, if any, believed
his claim that he had come to his controversial new con-
clusions after reappraisal of historical facts.

But even for the regime his conversion was not enough.

He had to repent in public; he had to interview, and some claimed even interrogate, other repentant political prisoners on television. Overnight he became a Judas. While the opposition thirsted for his martyrdom, the regime demanded his servility. Neither could tolerate a simple change of heart or mind. Then, as now, the cunning of politics haunted nearly all intellectual discourse in Iran.

Ironically, Nik-khah was one of the first people executed by the Islamic Republic. Once again, in his trial, he took the offensive. He talked of his fundamental philosophical disagreement with a theocratic state. He valiantly defended his political convictions of the past. But this time, nobody came to his defense. The royalists had never fully trusted him; the opposition had never forgiven him.

The rapid economic changes that seemed to have caused a change of heart in Nik-khah, augmented in the early seventies by the rapid rise of oil revenues, also changed the fabric of the capital. Tehran became a veritable El Dorado. Foreign heads of states and Iranian peasants, deposed monarchs and profit-hungry Western businessmen, Spiro Agnew out to broker a deal, and poor Indian engineers out to make a living, all converged on the city. The regime's grandiosity was as inflated as the price of land and the cost of living in Tehran.

Yet in those days Tehran suffered from cultural and economic incongruence; rather than one city, it had become a quilt of discordant communities. There was an unbreachable economic divide. On one side, fortunes of truly fantastic proportions had been amassed. A whole class of new moneyed socialites, addicted to conspicuous consumption, had turned large tracts of the city into rows of gaudy, gigantic mansions. While old money families of the city had historically tried to hide their affluence, the new wealthy class of corrupt government func-tionaries, contractors, and a few industrialists had as much desire to accumulate wealth as to display it. I loved to feel like a pariah among them. Land speculation and finan-cial and sexual contests and conquests seemed the only subjects that animated their conversations. Another favorite topic was the shortage of "reliable domestic help." They spoke nostalgically of the old days when ser-vants knew their places.

The Shahanshahi freeway was, to me, a metaphor for the corruption of this class. It had been one of Tehran's first freeways, connecting the sparsely populated upper class neighborhoods to the heart of the city. Other more populated areas of the capital remained quagmires of hor-rendous traffic jams. Many fortunes were made by those privy to the precise route of the future freeway. The royal family was said to have been the greatest beneficiary.

But just before the freeway ended at a large square, it made a very sharp turn. I almost wrecked my car the first time I tried to negotiate my way out of the loop. Others were less lucky. Scores of people had died in fatal accidents there. That loop had come to be called "the general's bend." To save his land from being condemned as public domain, a powerful general had forced a last minute change in the lay of the freeway.

Corruption was not the only fault of that avaricious class. Disdaining everything Iranian was another fad. For many, Persian had become synonymous with all that was abject, deceitful, and retrograde, and they distanced themselves from the very culture they were born into and now felt superior to. For them, Western culture was irresistibly alluring. Today much of this group lives in exile. Now they yearn for the very things they so recently despised. Around them a whole nostalgia industry has grown, creating, packaging, and reproducing the sounds, smells, and tastes of Iran.

Meanwhile, millions of villagers of yesterday had converged on the city in search of their fortune, and instead joined the ranks of millions more poorly housed, underemployed, disgruntled citizens. Disillusioned as they were, they became the warriors of the future revolution. Their lives were no doubt better than their fathers', but their rising expectations had far outpaced the meager improvement in their standards of living. In them, a new sense of entitlement had been created by the Pahlavi regime, and when the regime failed to deliver, they rebelled.

Parallel to this economic schism, a moral fault line had divided the city. On one side were the moderns who had embraced a new ethic of social behavior, a new dress code. A far larger group was only interested in salvation, which meant controlled sexuality and women who were sequestered at home and veiled in public. While the moderns looked condescendingly upon the traditionalists, a volatile mixture of resentment, desire, and hatred characterized the response of the traditionalists. Liberated women were portents of the apocalypse. "It's in the Book," an elderly aunt of mine used to say. "When men begin to look like women, when women openly mix and frolic with men, Imam's arrival is imminent."

Yet nothing in those days had prepared us for what now seems to have been historically inevitable. Technocrats like those in the queen's think tank often assumed secularization to be a more or less accomplished fact, and modernization a panacea to all social ills. As a political force and foe, religion was at best an insignificant nuisance. At the same time, opponents like Hamid and myself were infused with Marxian ideas about religion as the opiate of the people. To us religion was at best an instrument that could be used in our fight for liberation.

————————— A Season In Hell —————————

By the end of my second year in Tehran, my ritual every morning and many times during the night was to look outside and survey the cars parked in the neighborhood. In politically oppressive societies paranoia is one of the smaller prices one pays for political activism. Nothing is coincidental. Every gesture, every move, every anomaly, and every event is a moment of grand, woeful design, and a potential source of danger. But all seemed safe that morning. The last few patches of blue sky were giving way to threatening gray clouds. Snow seemed imminent.

I had to be at the minister's house by eight. Many members of his think tank were now undersecretaries in the Ministry of Education. I had been offered a similar position and refused. By then I was already trying to disengage myself, and I participated in fewer and fewer of the group's functions. That morning we were to make a surprise visit to a school principal in the poorest section of Tehran who was reportedly pilfering the government-allotted student lunch fund.

The minister lived in an ornately handsome house, incongruent with the squalor of its once aristocratic neighborhood. The newly wealthy and some of the old-moneyed families of Tehran had moved to new suburbs, showplaces for gaudy and gothic architecture and marble-mania, while the sudden convergence of millions of people on Tehran, searching for their share of the petro dollar, turned more and more of the "urb" and its distinguished old neighborhood into a ghetto.

In the old days Samad's store was half a block from where the minister lived. What Fauchon is to gastronomy today, Samad was then to fruits and vegetables. The aristocracy, oblivious of cost and particular in their taste, shopped there. Others bought there for social status. Gas lights illuminated Samad; it was the most beautiful store of my childhood. The proprietor's cherubic face belied his cunning. Samad used no price tags, but charged what the customer would bear. When bananas were an oddity in Iran and strawberries a rare delicacy, I remember

Samad's display of them by the colorful crate. The advent of supermarkets brought his demise. In place of his shop now stood a fifteen-story glass and steel high-rise, the national headquarters for Iran-Japan bank. I passed it on my way to the minister's house.

He greeted me in his usual congenial manner and ordered some tea. Before it arrived, the phone rang. He answered, exchanged the routine greetings, then just listened, losing color by the second. Finally he said, "Yes, his first name is Abbas," and after a bewildered glance at me, "Yes, he was educated in America, but it can't be him." Another pause, this time much longer. He promised to keep in touch. I was terrified.

In a voice more anguished than angry, he said, "It was from the security police. Your name has come up in connection with an opposition group. It isn't true, is it?"

With the bitter taste of fear puckering my mouth, soaked in cold perspiration, I mustered enough composure to deny the accusation. But I was already resigned to what I knew my fate would be.

The inspection at the high school lasted nearly four hours. We returned to the minister's office around noon. He told me he had arranged for me to meet with the head of internal security. "Be back by three," he said.

I walked to his secretary's office to ask for a car. While I waited, two men entered. One of them whispered something to the secretary, and a couple of minutes later she told me my car was ready. When I left the room, the two men followed.

Outside, a heavy snow had begun. I climbed into the blue Chevrolet and gave the driver the address where I wished to go. As soon as he pulled outside the iron gates of the ministry, we were surrounded by a half dozen cars. Security forces in civilian clothes, brandishing their Uzis, rushed the Chevrolet as the driver grabbed my arms. Someone opened the car door and forcefully stuck his two hands into my mouth to hold it open in case I was carrying a cyanide pill and would kill myself before his superiors had their day with me.

I was shoved into the back seat of a Volvo, a guard on either side of me. In that flicker of a moment before they pushed my head down between my knees and pulled my jacket over my back, I saw the bewildered face of a bystander, and the pity so prominent in his eyes reminded me of religious occasions during my childhood, watching the slaughter of sacrificial lambs in our backyard. The car took off and one of the men sitting in front, clearly the commander of the crew, announced in his transmitter,

"This is Shabdiz. The subject is in custody." Not long after that announcement, a voice on the transistor called Shabdiz and commanded him to also arrest the wife of the subject. "Back-up units forthcoming," the voice said.

Fereshteh's arrest and the subsequent search of our house for possible caches of leaflets, banned books, or guns took a long time. They found nothing. All the while, I sat in the back seat of the Volvo, watching first the arrest of my innocent wife, and then the search of our apartment.

Only moments after their search, around five o'clock in the afternoon, we arrived at what had come to be called the *Komiteh*. The early evening gloom only exacerbated my sense of despair. Once inside the *Komiteh*'s big metal gates, the transmitter activated again. "Don't turn the subject in. Wait for further orders."

I, like others in the opposition, had by then heard of "safe houses" where no records of detention were kept and security forces could dispatch anyone into an abyss and add her or his name to the list of "the disappeared." The wait lasted an eternity. I remember the snowflakes seemed particularly graceful in their descent. While somewhere, unbeknownst to me, a bureaucrat who only knew me through the confessions wrung out of other prisoners, was deciding whether I should be filed away in some terminal "safe house," the crew of Shabdiz talked about soccer. "Turn him in," the voice finally said to my great relief, and thus began my six-month journey into the *Komiteh*.

The *Komiteh*, short for the Committee to Fight Terrorism, was composed of forces including SAVAK, the police, and other security agencies interested in keeping the monarchy safe from subversion. It was located in the heart of the old city, if the city can be said to have a heart at all. The prison proper was part of a larger government complex that also housed the Department of Deeds and Records, infamous in Iran for its Chekhovian bureaucrats. The brick building with the facade of a palace in Persepolis was designed in the early part of the century when the cult of Aryan supremacy was in vogue. Visitors, a rarity in the *Komiteh*, and the interrogators both used the benign entrance of the Department of Deeds and Records to enter the prison.

The inconspicuous iron gate of this urban purgatory opened to a bustling Romanesque square where a petro-crazed economy thrived. Fruit juice kiosks, baked-potato stands, street hawkers and vendors shouting their wares, and beggars in search of alms crowded the square. Opposite the prison's iron gate was Tehran's central post office building. All around it sat scribes; men sitting on their tiny stools, pen and paper in hand, occasionally a typewriter by one foot, waiting for anyone from the illiterate multitude who had come to El Dorado and now wished to write home. Such scribes also acted as de facto attorneys, composing affidavits and petitions or any other official document for which the customer was willing to pay. I had often walked around the square in apprehension and happiness, dreading what I knew would be my inevitable entrance through that infamous gate, at the same time rejoicing that I was still free. While an inferno of suffering inflicted by men on men existed behind the iron gates, outside, life went on.

I was blindfolded in the car and led to a room where all my personal belongings, including my glasses, were packed away in a brown bag. I was issued a gray, shapeless cotton uniform, with a shin-high pair of pants—hardly an adequate defense against the bitter cold of Tehran's winters. Even the sight of my own ludicrous attire could not lighten the weight of fear and despair that had crept over me.

I was brought to the office of the head interrogator. A burly man, with tiny shifty eyes sunk deep into the fat layers of his face, told me not of my rights under the law but of the pain he could inflict upon me if I chose to be intransigent. Mixed with his threats were caustic remarks about my flimsy attire and how in his youth, professors used to dress with dignity.

"We know everything," he said. "Your job is only to confess." It did not take me long to realize that his pronouncement was no bluff. Clearly our circle was infested with infiltrators. In fact, one of the leaders of our circle, I soon learned, had been an agent of the regime all along.

Nahavandi had returned to Iran at the end of the sixties and was arrested soon thereafter. He was reported to have been brutally tortured in prison. Authorities took him to an army hospital from which he escaped. He joined the underground struggle almost immediately. With great fanfare, he published a pamphlet about his days in prison and the bright future of the struggle. But in fact the whole escape had been a set up and the pamphlet was a lie. Nahavandi had become an agent of SAVAK and at their behest had begun to throw a net to catch as many opponents of the regime as possible. He had gone about his work with the thoroughness of a compulsive manager. He preached the rhetoric of revolution and then reported every last person who ever stopped to listen.

It would be easy to claim that my decisions in prison were driven by the devastating realization of Nahavandi's betrayal, but my resistance had been broken long before this discovery. I had known for a while that I could not kill or die for an idea. The lure of ideology, once the beacon of my life, had lost its luster for me. Even before my arrest I had come to know that the game of power, and all the brutality it entails, was not for me. I had told Hamid that a simple teacher's life was what I had come to crave. He dismissed my suggestion, attributing it to a temporary lapse of resolve and to frayed nerves. The temporary lapse proved permanent, yet, for the stray walk I had taken, here was partial penance.

The meeting with the head interrogator lasted about half an hour. An old man was also present. He introduced himself as Colonel Zamani, infamous in our circles for his brutality as an interrogator. For almost the whole half hour, he sat silently and observed me. His silence was no less chilling than the threats made by Azodi, the head interrogator. He insisted on my guilt and asked about some trips I had made to meet other members of the opposition. I denied any complicity, hoping to buy some time and try to figure out what they in fact knew. When I told him that the trip was not political in purpose, but the result of a fight I had had with my wife, Azodi angrily got up from his chair, walked over, bent over to face me eye to eye, and as he punched me in chest, said, "You are in the *Komiteh* now. One way or the other, I'll make you talk." In the past eighteen years, rarely has there been a day or night in which the memory of his threats, his punch, and the fierce look in his eyes has not haunted me.

"Take this fool away," he told the guard he had called in. The man led me to a yard, by then veiled in darkness and covered with snow. He stood me outside a door, facing the wall. There were others waiting. No one dared utter a word. The piercing cold only added to the agony of the wait. I remembered the alcove under one of the staircases in our home when I was a child. It was a room without windows, dark and damp, essentially used for coal storage. In the summers, before refrigerators came to Iran, it was also used as a natural cooler. For the brave, it was a haven in our games of hide and seek; but the room had yet another function. If we misbehaved, we were banished there, forced to wait for a parental pardon. Maybe I owe my phobia of darkness to an early exile in that sooty alcove. One of the warmest memories of my childhood is of myself doing time in that infamous jail frightened and weeping, and my sister, the soulmate of my childhood, who came to me and said she would do time with me and keep me company.

Someone grabbed my hands and pulled me out of the cold into a room. He hung a number around my neck, someone else took my picture, and soon thereafter I was led to face my interrogator.

The interrogators were either called "doctor" or went by a chosen first name. One was Kaveh, another went by the name of Arash; both are names of heroes of Iranian mythology. Mine called himself Dr. Majidi. He fancied himself an intellectual. He was a hypochondriac, constantly gulping pills. Once he had me translate the label of one of the medications he was taking. With trepidation I explained that it was a hormonal equalizer, suggested for women in menopause. "That's nonsense," he said. "My doctor says it's good for nerves."

On the eve of the Revolution he and several other interrogators were arrested while most of their superiors escaped to safe havens abroad. In a public trial, he was sentenced to fifteen years in prison. But then the Islamic Republic came under intense pressure to find and punish the culprits in an infamous act of arson.

A few months before, the doors to the Rex Theater in the city of Abadan had been locked from the outside, the building drenched in flammable liquids and then set on fire. Six hundred people burned to their deaths. Rumors connected some of the top clerics of Iran to the crime. Arson, people said, had been used to provoke anger and rebellion in the populace. One fact seems incontrovertible. In the chronology of events leading to the Islamic Revolution, the arson at the Rex Theater played a singularly important role and had a catalytic effect in radicalizing the people. And after the Revolution, rumors about clerical responsibility for the fire continued to grow. To quell these, a number of already imprisoned security forces, including Dr. Majidi, were summarily tried and executed on charges of arson. But rumors of clerical complicity only intensified after the trial.

After my picture was taken and I was led to Majidi's office, my blindfold was lifted. There was a small metal desk in one corner of the room and an army cot, neatly made, in the other. A picture of the shah hung on the wall. On the bed, I could see an old brown suitcase. Majidi began by introducing himself. After his name, the first thing he told me were the names of famous intellectuals he had interrogated in the past. He then informed me that he knew everything he needed to know about my case. There was no escape from punishment, and the severity of that punishment, he said, would depend on my honesty in answering his questions.

He would write each question on a legal pad and wait for me to write my answer; then he would read my response and ask another question. The first few questions were formalities about my name and address. He then asked about any connection I might have had to any member of the opposition. As I began to write, he moved to where the suitcase had been, opened it, and with decided nonchalance, began to browse through its contents. Clearly, he meant for me to see the piled documents. I recognized the pamphlets and leaflets we had written against the shah and his regime. Halfheartedly, I denied any connection to anyone in the opposition and Majidi read my denial with a smirk on his face and occasional verbal threats.

He asked me about the trip I had taken two weeks earlier to the city of Kermanshah, then a hotbed of radical Kurdish activity. I repeated my sorry tale about the fight I had had with my wife and about my desire to get away. This time he pretended to be particularly angry and said my stupidity and intransigence would not only add to my own troubles but would complicate my wife's case as well. I knew I would have to confess. I was only trying to buy more time.

Around four in the morning, Dr. Majidi called a break

in the interrogation and I was taken to my cell. A tin bowl of soup, topped by a white layer of congealed fat, and a piece of bread awaited me. Spoons were not allowed in cells; a security precaution, they said, to save the lives of prisoners. It would be a fortnight before I would again use a utensil.

Hunger had devoured my appetite. The room was small: three short steps in width, five in length. The only source of light was a small electric bulb, in a dust-ridden, grated metal net that hung outside the cell, shedding its dim light through an opening at the top of the white, metal door. A stained, filthy carpet covered the floor. Two army blankets served as my mattress, pillow, and cover. There was a small fenced and barred window on the wall facing the door, near the ceiling, beyond reach. What it opened to I never discovered, but for only about an hour in the early afternoon, a thin, often lackluster ray of sun fought its way into that awful place and connected me to the elements.

I spent two restless hours there. Around six in the morning, a guard took me again to the head interrogator's office. The minute my blindfold was lifted, Azodi began his verbal barrage. He had my interrogation sheets in his hands. Waving them in the air, he said, "You son of bitch, what kind of nonsense is this. I tried to give you a break. I told you we know everything, and you repay me with this garbage."

He tore to pieces everything I had written last night and made a pledge, pointing to the picture of the king, "I swear by his sacred crown that I will have you and your wife executed." He was shouting at the top of his lungs.

The phone rang. "Yes sir," he said calmly, with no hint of anger in his voice.

"He is here," he went on. He listened for a few seconds and then gestured me to the phone. Sabeti, one of the most feared and efficient heads of SAVAK was on line. He told me that I was being a fool, that my influential uncles or friends could do nothing to help me, and that full and truthful confession was the only solution. He then asked me to put Azodi back on the line.

By the time he put down the receiver, Azodi's tone of voice had completely changed. He ordered me a tea and asked whether I needed anything before going back to the interrogator's office. I said I wanted to see my wife.

A few minutes later the door to Azodi's office opened. A guard led Fereshteh in. She groped around, trying to avoid the furniture. Upon arrest her much-needed eye glasses had been taken away. The sight of her groping, of her threadbare uniform and her disheveled look brought tears to my eyes and Azodi noticed, saying in a tone that combined an implicit threat with a compliment, "We won't have any problems with you. Anyone who can cry for his wife cannot be a terrorist." I spent a precious couple of minutes with Fereshteh and then we each went to our separate interrogator's office. I had by then resolved to confess to my own misdeeds, but not provide any information that could potentially cause someone else's arrest.

I spent the next five hours in Majidi's office. Around noon I was taken back to my cell. There was a small hole in the metal door, covered from outside by a sliding piece of metal. It was usually locked. Once an hour, the guard on duty slid the metal door open and peeped in. If the guards should forget to lock the cover, as they sometimes did, then the metal could be pushed aside from inside the cell and one could dare a glance of the hall.

My first attempt to catch such a glance was a disaster. I had hardly slid the metal piece from inside when the guard opened the door and kicked and punched me for my offense.

The hall was long and dimly lit. Our only source of heat was a loud electrical heater located near the center. The *Komiteh* was notorious for being too cold in the winter and unbearably hot in the summer. The hall was hauntingly silent, pierced only occasionally by a moan more haunting than the silence it broke.

I spent three weeks in solitary confinement. No reading material was permitted. Days or nights not spent in the torment of interrogation were spent on the enervating task of finding ways to break the monotony, to cure loneliness, and in ever-persistent process of self-examination and doubt. I worried about my parents and their reaction to my arrest. I anguished about my wife. I was tormented by the possible fate of Vaez-zadeh and other people in our circle.

Toilets were located at the end of the hall. Prisoners were taken there at three designated times of the day. Only rare emergencies warranted the luxury of an extra visit to the bathroom. Several weeks passed before soap and towels appeared in our toilets.

Public toilets in Iran, usually consisting of a hole atop a septic tank, are notoriously dirty and foul-smelling. The toilets in the *Komiteh* were always meticulously clean. Toilets and halls (and our dishes) were cleaned and washed every night by prisoners. It was a much coveted job, for it afforded not only a few minutes outside the claustrophobic enclosure of a cell, but also a chance to tap into the prison grapevine.

One hot topic those days was the gradual and gratifying changes that had begun to appear in the life of the *Komiteh*. Soap and towels in toilets, spoons in cells, hotter tea in the morning, and even less torture. The changes, we all knew, had to do with American politics. Carter had just been elected president. While I do not know how history will judge his presidency, I know that because of his human rights policy, I, and many like me, were spared much suffering, and for this I will always be grateful.

My defenses against the cold, weak since my childhood, broke down by the second day of my incarceration and by the third day my fever was deemed high enough by the interrogator to warrant a visit to the infirmary. The will and whim of the interrogator dominated every facet of prisoners' lives.

My blindfold was lifted once I was inside the white-tiled hall of the prison hospital. An awful odor, private odors of human suffering mixed with the sterile smell of chloroform, filled the air. There was a heap of bloodied bandages on the right side of the hall where wounds on tortured limbs were dressed to prepare them for further suffering. The sight reminded me of Dante's Inferno. It was at once repulsive, abhorrent, and frightening. Past visitors to this infirmary, whose bandages were a token of their indescribable suffering, were often forced to choose their torture. The menu was long: flogging, arm twisting, cigarette burning, crucifixion, sleep deprivation, electric shock, fingernail pulling, genital crushing, genital electric shock, hook-hanging, needles pushed under finger nails, and finally the Apollo. In America, the Apollo space program was a symbol of the spirit of the "new frontier," a metaphor for the conquests of humanity and science. In the *Komiteh* it meant a metal hood placed on the head of a prisoner that would amplify the sound of his shrieks when he was flogged. The result was deafening by the sound of one's own suffering.

The chief executioner of this menu, the exorcist of information and confession, was a man named Hosseini. On the third day of my interrogation, burning with fever, I sat in the interrogator's office, answering the same question for maybe the tenth time. They wanted to know the identity and the description of the person I had met when I had traveled to Kermanshah. That was one of the few things they did not know about our activity. Hoping to avoid the arrest of yet another group like ourselves, I had not given them accurate information about my contacts in that city. Instead, I concocted an imaginary character

149

and described him every time Majidi asked me about him. Interrogators believed that repetition would betray fabricated stories. Inconsistencies in answers to the same question was a sign of lying. I was desperately combing my mind to remember every detail of what I had said before, when a pinched nerve in my shoulder caused me to turn in sudden pain. I found myself facing a lanky, much-aged man whose terrible empty gaze shriveled the spirit.

"I am Hosseini," he said in a shrill voice, and added menacingly, "I think you have heard of me." Indeed I had. But all I had heard had not prepared me for the terror of his presence and the almost palpable air of cruelty he exuded. Was it the face that had driven him to his profession, or was it the profession that had created such a monstrous persona?

When the Islamic Revolution began to dispense its version of revolutionary justice, Hosseini was one of the earliest victims. Among all the accused, he seemed to be the most ready to die, almost already dead.

Village Prison

The little aperture in my cell occasionally afforded me a glance at the pale reflection of a sun making its graceful appearance near the ceiling. The only feast of light came a couple of days before my trial, in the fourth month of my imprisonment. By then there were eleven of us in my cell. Shortly before my arrest, at the behest of SAVAK, daily newspapers had announced that eleven opponents of the regime had been arrested and would soon be tried. It mattered little that at the time of the announcement I was not yet under arrest. Even less important, apparently, the eleven of us in that room, destined to stand trial together, had not even been part of the same circle. The government wanted a trial of eleven people and we were the chosen ones. Prison life invariably vacillates between the torments of solitude or the suffocation of overcrowded cells.

It was Friday, usually the quietest day at the *Komiteh*, when around ten, the door to our cell was flung open. We were ordered to put on our blindfolds. Then in a single line, each prisoner holding onto a piece of the uniform of the person in front of him, we were led to where we immediately felt fresh air, a sharp contrast with the mildewed atmosphere of our cells.

"Take off your blindfolds," our guard said.

We found ourselves near the dust-ridden metal balustrade that circled a third-story balcony. We were informed we had been allotted fifteen minutes of sun. This was the interrogators' idea of a cosmetic cure for our pallor. The approach was not all that different from how the old regime coped with nearly all of its social problems. I remember specifically a visit by Queen Elizabeth in my childhood, for which all the walls along the road from the airport to her designated residential palace were freshly painted. Streets were repaved, flowers and greens were planted—an urban facelift was performed. This practice was repeated every time a significant foreign luminary came to visit. Maybe that is why so many analysts and policy-makers, Iranians and Westerners alike, were shocked at the flimsiness of what had seemed like

the solid foundation of the Pahlavi regime. Facades sometimes take on the authority of facts, even in the minds of
their architects.

But on that Friday morning, our only interest was to
devour as much of the sun as possible. Like the dead
emerging from Hades, we clustered in a small sun-
bathed corner, wishing that time would take longer than
usual to pass.

Two days later our trial began. In those days, most
political trials were conducted in secret. Ours was to be a
public affair. Our case had attracted much publicity in the
West. Those pressures, as well as President Carter's influence, had made it necessary for the shah's regime to
improve its dismal human rights record. Our trial was to
be part of this endeavor. I, as well as others in that group
of eleven, engaged in what in the parlance of legal practice would be called a plea bargain. In the purist vocabulary of political radicalism, our decision was derided as
an act of compromise and a sign of weakness. But by then
I didn't care. I wanted to find an honorable way to pay
the price I knew I must pay to regain my freedom.

I agreed not to criticize the regime during the trial, in
return for the promise to be released in a year. I was
indeed pardoned in eleven and a half months. But then

when the mass media reported my testimony in court, they turned what had been a plea for constitutional rights into an oration in praise of the king.

The trial and the appeal process took a couple of months and resembled a farcical rendition of a tragedy. We were tried by a military tribunal. A lean, somber-faced general presided and two other colonels completed the panel. Our court-appointed attorney was more malicious in his defense than the prosecutor was in his indictment. Our lawyers were unequivocal about our guilt. They only pleaded for leniency, and their pleas were based on what one of them caustically called the ignorance of our youth. The fact that all but one of the eleven defendants were from the ranks of the highly educated, foreign-trained professional class was no deterrence to his strategy, and he was particularly sarcastic when referring to the one manual laborer in our group—our token proletariat. He talked of the man's undeniable stupidity. In a tone of sarcasm and condescension, he pointed to the poor man and asked the tribunal, "How can you punish such an imbecile?"

Even the plush surroundings of the courtroom could not hide the banality of the exercise. The defendants, the judges, the prosecutor, and the attorneys, as well as the few spectators and journalists permitted in the spacious but otherwise empty room, all knew that this was no trial but a show of marionettes with SAVAK pulling the strings and an amorphous "Western public opinion" the sole spectator. When the show finally ended, I and the other ten in our group were taken to Evin prison, on the outskirts of Tehran. By then I had spent six months in the *Komiteh*.

My wife was the only member of my family present at the trial. She had been set free after forty-five days in prison. After her release, I had seen her only twice. Visitors were usually not allowed in the *Komiteh*. I had seen my father once. My family had pulled many strings to arrange these visits. My mother had refused to come. "I will never visit my son in a prison," she said, and she kept her promise. My father did come, and was visibly shaken when he saw me in prison uniform. The meeting was in the head interrogator's office. My father was sitting on a couch as I entered, and he began to sob. He cried as I have never seen him do before or since. I sat by him, kissed and held his hands and tried to reassure him. He mustered few words. Later, I heard from my brother Hossein that on that day, from where he had parked his car to the office, a distance of two blocks, my father had stopped five times to urinate. In Evin prison, visits were more regular and less traumatic.

Evin was once an idyllic little village perched on the footsteps of a towering mountain renowned for its crisp mountain air, fresh berries, and old walnut trees. A beautiful river carved its way through gigantic rocks, skirting the village and its lush orchards.

But then, beginning in the early sixties, the landscape of the village began to change. A private university, soon taken over by the government, was erected nearby. Hilton put its marble stamp on a hilltop near the village. Another luxury hotel, this one owned by the Pahlavi foundation and named Hotel Evin, rose around the bend of the dirt road leading to the village. A giant international fairground was constructed, and to complete the amenities of modernization, an eighteen-hole golf course, designed by one of the luminaries of the international golf circuit. Membership in the Royal Club was coveted by every genuine Iranian social climber in the seventies. And there was also Evin Prison, close enough to the Evin Hotel that on most summer nights we could hear the soft sound of dance music from the hotel gardens—a sound at once tantalizing and repulsive.

Our van passed the hotel, negotiated a dirt road, and soon reached a big metal gate, beyond which lay another narrow roadway that climbed past giant walnut trees.

What was now a prison had once been an orchard. In a quiet corner of that aging orchard sat an old building that was in those days a prison for women. Beyond it an electronic gate opened to a courtyard enclosed by high cement walls. The giant prison, modern, multi-leveled, with a red brick facade, sat ominously in the corner of that yard. Though only recently built, it had by then already developed a frightening reputation. There were rumors that it had been designed and constructed by the Israelis. On the eve of the Revolution, when the transition of power to the Islamic clerics was sealed with a popular uprising, people stormed Evin Prison.

When Bastille fell at the time of the French Revolution, no more than a handful of prisoners were found inside. By the time Evin was liberated, most of its political prisoners had already been set free by the government. Nevertheless, for days people sought catacombs from which they claimed to have heard the lingering moans of forgotten prisoners. No catacombs or forgotten prisoners were found, but government records soon showed that the prison had been built not by Israelis but by an Iranian architectural firm, renowned, ironically, for the progressive reputation of one of its senior partners.

The alleged complicity of Israelis in the construction

of the infamous prison was not the only instance where insidious foreign hands were blamed for Iranian problems. Both royalists and their foes liked to castigate "foreign devils" for society's woes. I remember when, a few weeks before the Revolution, soldiers opened fire on peaceful demonstrators in Jaleh square. Many of my friends seriously believed that American and Israeli soldiers had done the firing, insisting that "No Iranian soldier would do this."

A few weeks later, angry mobs goaded by radicals attacked army barracks, armed themselves, and went on to occupy several government offices. Royalists indignantly said, "Did you see the Palestinian terrorists brandishing their guns?" Gradually, and begrudgingly, we had to face the fact that both the angry mobs that disarmed the barracks and the frightened soldiers who had fired on unarmed civilians, and even the architect of Evin prison, were all Iranians.

But that day when the van stopped in front of the steps leading to the prison building, I was not considering the national identity of the prison's founders but my new circumstances.

While it was a great relief to leave the infamous *Komiteh*, I also felt an ambiguous sense of discomfort and disruption. The dark and mildewed atmosphere of the *Komiteh*, the long hours pacing in our small cells, our three-minute weekly showers, and even the petty cruelties of some of the guards had all, by then, become part of our routine, and there is comfort in routine. All that was about to change.

After the usual rituals of prison orientation, we were taken to cell block Number One. Our unit, like others at Evin, was two-tiered. A yellow metal door opened onto a gray, tiled landing. To the right, stairs led to the lower tier. All walls were pale yellow. At the end of the landing was an L-shaped, dimly-lit hallway with eight solid metal doors. The first three doors opened to cells. The last door on one side contained a small bath. From floor to ceiling, this room was cast in gray, coarse cement, with three shower heads protruding from the wall. The first room around the corner was where the toilets were located, then three more cells. Each cell was actually designed to hold eight people. In those days the number of occupants ranged from ten to sixty. Later, the Islamic Republic broke all records and reportedly crammed some hundred people into each cell.

The upper tier of our block, where the eleven of us shared a room, was renowned as a "select" unit set aside for clerics, famous intellectuals, and favored political prisoners. Some of the most powerful men in the Islamic Republic today were then inmates of cellblock Number One.

Cells were strictly segregated by ideology. Interestingly enough, it was the prisoners themselves who had opted for this. The fault line was religion. Secular prisoners lived with comrades of similar persuasion, while the pious communed with their brethren. In fact, all cells were organized as communes. Lonely were those few mavericks who chose to live outside the commune, or were banished from the collective on suspicions of dubious political connections or inclinations. The emotional violence they experienced—the menacing glances, mysterious rumors, and exclusion from social discourse—was often as cruel and inhuman as the physical and emotional violence unleashed by the police against the rest of us. In the caste society of the prison, those banished ones were the untouchables.

The communes had all the trappings of a strictly egalitarian structure. Everything was shared and shared equally. Provisions that visitors were permitted to bring for each prisoner, from fruits and cigarettes to books and magazines, went into a communal pool where they were then rationed among all members of each commune.

There was an equal division of labor as well. Each day, on a rotating basis, two or three prisoners performed all the work in the commune, arranging our communal breakfasts, lunches, and dinners. They cleaned the halls, tidied the cells, and washed the dishes. With a distinct sense of pride and purpose, they were "the workers of the block." In those days, "labor" still had a magical, messianic attraction for us. Mimicking a proletarian identity was the quintessential symbol of radicalism. In fact, hard work and diligence as a worker of the block was a sure sign of ideological purity. Only decadent petit bourgeois elements, we believed, scoffed at hard work for communal benefit.

Beneath this ostensible communalism existed a frighteningly strict, stratified, hierarchically organized and segregated reality that contradicted the appearance of equality. Power and information were unequally distributed. Important decisions were usually made by a few self-appointed leaders. Those were the days when the Chinese Cultural Revolution and the mystique of Castro and his guerrilla politics still had a strong presence in the minds of Iranian radicals. Thus, the amount of torture a prisoner had suffered, the years he had spent in prison, his unbending and periodically manifested antagonism toward the regime, his aversion to what was euphemistically and disdainfully called intellectualism, his commitment to ideological scrutiny by others and of others, and finally his willingness to play an active role in the machinations of the inner power structure were all factors determining the political status of each prisoner. Often what was held out as ideological criticism was nothing more than petty, oppressive, and intense gossip about some insignificant aspect of a comrade's behavior. I saw men who had by then spent a decade of their lives in prison because of their commitment to a revolutionary ideology, who still argued, ad nauseam, about the moral failings of a comrade who had taken too big a bite from a shared lunch plate. While wide vistas and an open horizon seem to broaden our vision and bring out the poet and the prophet in us, the claustrophobic enclosures of prison and the grueling monotony of its routine limited our sensibility.

Needless to say, nearly all of this bickering was put forth as ideological struggle. There was a sense of perpetual and pervasive mutual scrutiny, and the scrutiny was the strictest when it came to the question of sex. A major moral crisis erupted in cellblock Number One when an inmate, a proletarian poet, made a passing comment about the bosom of a certain actress. Days were spent analyzing the responsibilities of political prisoners and the impropriety of comments that could be even remotely construed as erotically suggestive. While the regime was said to be adding saltpeter to our food in prison, our self-imposed code of conduct further contributed to tame our sexual inclinations. This sexual Puritanism had one redeeming quality. Because of it, political prisoners were spared the agonies of sexual harassment by other inmates, a common pestilence of prison life. Of all political prisoners in those days, only one was said to have made a rebuffed advance on another young inmate, and he, ironically, became for a short while the Republic's Minister of Islamic Guidance.

It took me a while to recognize how champions of liberty and equality had helped create a small emotional gulag in prison, and how social life among us was fraught with nuances of inequality and hierarchy, but I quickly learned the serious segregated nature of my new milieu.

On my first full day at Evin, I woke early, the nervous waking in a new abode. I was pacing the short length of the landing when the door opened. A guard clumsily pushed four partially soot-covered, much-dented kettles of luke-warm tea into the landing. Bread and feta cheese completed our breakfast ration. A number on each kettle indicated the room it belonged to. Having met the elder clerics from rooms four and five the night before, I decided, in deference to their age, to deliver their kettles to them.

As I turned from the landing into the long hall, one of the more seasoned prisoners saw me and apprehensively told me to quickly put their kettles back where I had found them. "They don't like us to touch their things," he said.

His advice came too late. By then one of the clerics had turned the corner and saw my sinful hands on their kettles. Feigning indifference, he took the kettles and went back to their rooms. We soon heard about a turmoil in their commune, a heated debate about whether a cup of tea from a kettle carried by the hands of a suspected infidel is *najes*, unclean. All but one member of the religious commune had apparently refused to drink the tea. Although the tea itself had not been touched by the poisoned hands of an infidel, caution counseled against the suspicious kettle and its contents. I remember my feelings—a combination of condescension, slight sense of insult, self-congratulatory righteousness, and finally pity for what I considered their anachronist gesture. When, in a couple of years, those same presumably marginalized cell mates seized power and mobilized enormous mass sup-

port for their ways and values, my sense of insult gave way
to one of fear, estrangement, and deep doubts about my
understanding of at least some aspects of Iranian society.

That day the one dissenting voice had been Ayatollah
Taleqani's. He was a legend in modern Iranian politics,
one of that rare breed whose reputation among his peers
was as solid as his fame among the populace. By the time
I met him in Evin, he had been in and out of prison for
nearly half a century. His white beard, the compassion in
his eyes, and the white cotton pants and long tunics he
wore gave him a saintly aura. Other clerics also wore such
apparel, which set them apart from the rest of us in the
common gray prison uniforms. As in society, so in prison,
the mullahs persisted in promoting an image of authority.

Ayatollah Taleqani negotiated his way around the halls
or the yard in a cautious graceful manner, almost gliding,
with no abrupt movements of his head or hands, always
aware of the eyes that watched him. Of all the clerics, he
spent the most time with the non-religious prisoners,
clearly relishing the respect he enjoyed among prisoners from all sides of the political spectrum. He was a master of gestures at once subtle and safe that conveyed his
differences with the more traditional clerics and yet did
not offend their sense of solidarity and propriety.

I remember one winter afternoon pacing with him up and down the narrow hallway of our block. "Too old to fight the cold," he had said. In the third room on our side of the wing, a television was on. The Islamists had no televisions in their rooms. For them it was a sacrilege to look at the unveiled face of a woman even on a television screen. Yet, each time we passed the room with the television, the old man slowed his pace, and wary of other pious eyes, peered through the small opening in the door and watched the screen for a moment. When I suggested a short rest in the television room, he answered coyly, "That wouldn't be a good idea. You know how they are."

When, on the dawn of the Revolution, his popularity soared to unparalleled heights, some of his clerical critics accused him of being used and manipulated by the opposition. Others began to doubt the sincerity of his political tolerance. "He lusts for power and craves popularity," some said. His rift with Ayatollah Khomeini and other prominent clerics on the one hand, and his vacillation on the question of waning civil liberties on the other, began to undermine his popular image. His death, not long after, was rumored to be the result of foul play.

Ayatollah Taleqani's unmatched political stature, experience, and popularity was not equal to his status among the clerics. Shiite clerics are notorious for their sensitivity to the question of hierarchy. In fact, there is a labyrinthine system of ranks, titles, and rituals that determines each mullah's place in the pious pecking order. It has been suggested, wisely I think, that one reason the Islamic government never succeeded in its goal of a monolithic theocracy has been the obsessive preoccupation of each of the clerics with their place in the hierarchy and their almost invariable refusal to accept the higher authority of any another clergy. Their jealous guardianship of this hierarchy, as well as the mullah's mastery of the art of symbolic politics, has resulted in elaborate, minutely detailed yet rigorously enforced rules of etiquette about everything from seating in a gathering of clerics to the titles that must be used in addressing each member of the caste. Understanding the rudiments of these rules, we had an occasion to see the inner hierarchy of our clerical cell mates in action.

It was the last day of Ramadan, traditionally a rare day of festivities for Shiites. For the truly pious, of course, nothing is more joyous than prayer itself. Thus the clerics had asked prison authorities for permission to hold a public prayer in the prison yard. In the past no such rituals had been permitted in Evin. But there was now a new atmosphere of tolerance in prison. We knew that prison policies invariably reflected political developments in society at large. This new policy reflected Carter's insistence on human rights. When the clerics' request was granted, we knew that a new stage in Iranian politics was about to begin. Nevertheless, I doubt that on that day, anyone, including the most militant and optimistic clerics, could have guessed that in less than three years, most of those gathered in the yard to perform their public prayer would be the ruling elite of Iran.

The rest of us gathered behind the barred, mesh-screened window of the second floor not only to watch the spectacle but also to get a clear clue as to who was the highest ranking cleric in the group. We knew that this would be the man who would lead the public prayer.

Ayatollah Taleqani was in the front line. Next to him stood Ayatollah Montazeri. To his right was Mahdavi Kani, destined to become a caretaker prime minister of the Islamic Republic. Lahouti, later chosen as the first commander of the now-powerful Revolutionary Guards and famous in prison as a dandy, obsessed with the fine trim of his beard, stood to the left of Taleqani. After a few seconds of mutual deference, it was Ayatollah Montazeri who finally took a short step forward and led the public prayer for the day.

Montazeri had been a student and a close confidant of Ayatollah Khomeini. After the victory of the Islamic Revolution, upon designating his disciple as his chosen successor, Ayatollah Khomeini said of Montazeri, "He is the fruit of my life." Later, when Montazeri went too far in criticizing some of the oppressive policies of his patron-patriarch, he was not only summarily stripped of all position and power, but was accused of gullibility and ignorance.

In fact, Ayatollah Montazeri met his demise in the crossfire of the Iran-Contra affairs. It was a member of his staff who first leaked the story of the clandestine "arms for hostages" deal to a Lebanese newspaper. When the Islamic regime retaliated by arresting and eventually executing the whistle blower, Montazeri became particularly vociferous in his criticism of the regime for which he was then the chosen successor. When the rift became public he was put under house arrest and eventually stripped of all official positions.

Though a passionate and persistent believer, Montazeri had become a political liability. He was an odd duck even in his prison days. He wore the hem of his pants tucked into the top of his socks, and cavorted around the halls in a manner incongruent with his age. He spent much of his time reading and rereading religious texts. He was also learning English then. An English translation of the Koran by a Pakistani Muslim was his text of choice. I was his occasional English tutor. It was hard not to be amused by his attempt at the English language, which he spoke with a heavy peasant accent.

In those days, those of us with a sense of historical and moral self-righteousness and intellectual superiority looked condescendingly at Ayatollah Montazeri and others like him. While he apparently chose to forgive these affronts, one of his spiritual brethren of those days was less forgiving.

His name was Lajevardi. As chief prosecutor for the Revolutionary Tribunal, he gained notoriety as the butcher of Tehran. He was awful to look at, his face ravaged by a pitiless disease, probably small pox. Perhaps his soul, too, was devastated by the tortures he suffered in prison and the humiliation he must have felt in a world that seemed to become more and more hostile to his beliefs.

Under the old regime, he had been imprisoned several times, once for his role in blowing up the offices of El Al in Tehran. He was a lonely man in prison, often reading the Koran and occasionally talking to his one and only friend, an unknown and inexperienced teacher who went on to become a controversial prime minister in the Islamic Republic. In spite of his self-created isolation, Lajevardi was at times drawn into heated ideological debates. He was cursed with an unfailing memory, and many of those who had disagreed with him later came to pay a heavy price for it.

As a powerful prosecutor and the ultimate dispenser of Islamic revolutionary justice, Lajevardi had a coterie of committed zealots. Together they sought, and often found and punished, the unfortunate infidels who in the old days had exhibited hubris in the eyes of God, his prophet, and his progeny. Shiite jurisprudence demands that each pious Muslim individually punish anyone he or she hears or sees engaged in a blasphemous act. This imminence of violence, individual or collective, in every observed breach of a major theological precept must be one of the more dangerous aspects of Shiite thought.

In the heyday of his power, Lajevardi and some of his Revolutionary Guards roamed the city in search of old political prisoners. It was even reported that they kept a constant watch around the toll gates to Tehran's freeways. I was frightened every time I came near those gates. When I moved to the San Francisco Bay area, I invariably had a sense of anxiety whenever I approached one of the bridges. It took me a while to recognize the source of my anxiety and even longer to free myself of it.

Lajevardi brought terror not only to the hearts of old political prisoners, but to the whole city of Tehran and to the very halls and rooms in which he was once incarcerated. By dawn, he might order the execution of several hundred youths, and by dusk of the same day, he would pick up a broom and in a gesture of compassion help the prisoners clean up their cells. No haughty prosecutor was he. In the post-revolutionary culture that praised poverty as virtue, he flaunted his humble credentials as one of the dispossessed every day.

His schizoid behavior had a solid historical genealogy. Shah Abbas, the pious king who consolidated Shiism as the official state religion of Iran, spent hours in mournful meditation, yet a group of cannibals, called the Chagari-e Battalion, stood at his side. At a mere gesture by the king, they would dismember and devour the king's enemies. Mullah Shafti, a nineteenth-century Shiite version of Lucrezia Borgia, amassed an enormous fortune from foreclosing on real estate he held as collateral for his usurious loans, though usury is a mortal sin in Islam. In the mid-nineteenth century, he was one of the most powerful clerics in the city of Isfahan. Disciples write of the fervor with which he decapitated anyone accused of membership in the Babi sect. They also write of the grief he would display for the deceased near their decapitated bodies, of his insistence on praying for their sins.

In the days of our incarceration, not all the clerics had the zealotry of Lajevardi. In fact many tried to keep their distance from the ideological fray. Rafsanjani was one such figure. I remember how surprised I was when in our first encounter, he told me of a visit with his children. He looked too young to have children.

As a short beardless man, Rafsanjani had to surmount a serious cultural obstacle. Beardless men are called *kuseh* in Persian. It is a word layered with connotations of calculated brutality, synonymous with a shark, a powerful adversary who creeps up quietly on his target and then with a sharp, determined move takes down the enemy. The last ruling *kuseh* in Iran was Agha Mohammed Khan, the founder of the Qajar dynasty in the eighteenth century, who helped forge national unity and end long years of internal strife. Yet he is notorious for his brutality. Apocryphal though the story may be, it is commonly believed that once, angered by the stare of an inhabitant of the city of Kerman, he ordered his soldiers to gouge out the eyes of forty thousand inhabitants of the unfortunate city.

In prison days, Rafsanjani was clearly a second-rank cleric. On the day of that public prayer in the prison yard, he stood on the second line. He was little known outside religious circles. Yet as a trusted disciple of Ayatollah Khomeini, he was catapulted into fame on the eve of the Revolution when he read an important proclamation of the patriarch in which the Ayatollah had, by revolutionary fiat, appointed a new provisional prime minister.

In prison, Rafsanjani was translating a book on the history of Palestine. He rarely emerged from his cell. He had a peculiarly light walk, catlike and quick. His face was devoid of expression; his eyes always looked tired. He mingled with the non-religious prisoners just enough not to appear prudishly pious, yet he had refused to drink that sullied tea. He was an avid listener and a cautious talker.

When the revolution came, he compensated for the stigma of being a *kuseh* and a cleric of low rank with patience and shrewd pragmatism. He also succeeded in orchestrating a centralist position for himself, transcending factional feuds and emerging as one of the most powerful figures in post-Khomeini Iran. Eclectic in matters of ideology and masterful in the art of double talk—a staple of all revolutions—he tried to articulate a voice of reason in the unreasonable milieu of revolutionary euphoria. To preserve his left flank, he never let up on his revolutionary rhetoric. At the same time, he called for moderation and realism. With the death of Khomeini, his rhetoric gradually gave way to realism. I got another close glimpse of his political style about seven years after our first encounter in prison.

It was the spring of 1984. A group of Muslim students, calling themselves the true "Followers of the Imam," had bullied their way into the office of the vice chancellor of Tehran University, accused the poor man of harboring liberal ideas, and physically assaulted him. We in the Faculty of Law sent a delegation to meet with Rafsanjani to voice our concern for the future of the university and to protest against acts of violence and disruption by Islamic students. Rafsanjani was then the powerful Speaker of the House. Though he was not directly involved with the management of the university, we had come to know him as a pillar of power, almost on a par with Ayatollah Khomeini himself, and a man more amenable to reason.

The delegation was composed of the dean of the faculty, the heads of each academic department, and myself.

"He might remember you and that would add a personal touch," my colleagues suggested.

What had once been the somber and silent Senate chamber of the ancient regime was now the seat of a cantankerous *Majlis*, a mullah-dominated House of Representatives. The presence of Revolutionary Guards throughout the building made the place seem like barracks rather than a parliament. We had all chosen to wear ties. By then, wearing a tie had become a defiant act. Ties were synonymous with decadent cosmopolitanism, a token of Westophilia.

At three different checkpoints, we were thoroughly, and at times contemptuously, frisked. Finally we were led to a waiting room. The furniture was meager by any standard, little wooden chairs stood against barren walls. A picture of Ayatollah Khomeini, his face stern, aged, and aloof, his eyes looking away from the camera, was the only adornment on the walls. There were also two gray metal desks in the room, cluttered with folders and envelopes. Behind each desk sat a bearded young man dressed in a baggy cotton shirt and plastic slippers. The beard, the shirt, and the slippers were in those days all signs of Islamic humility, emblems of a kind of folksy simplicity that often hid pure brutality.

We waited for about ten minutes. One of the two secretaries tried to explain the cause of the delay. "Brothers bound for the front are meeting him," he said. Finally, we were guided to an adjoining room. Behind a simple wooden desk stood Rafsanjani who greeted each of us politely with a handshake. His diminutive figure was clearly overshadowed by another giant picture of Ayatollah Khomeini, disdainfully gazing into the distance from a white makeshift wall, behind which a small, neatly made, single bed was visible. In those days, fear of assassins had made most of the ruling clerics prisoners of their offices.

The meeting began with the requisite formal introductions and greetings. When my turn came, Rafsanjani used a language at once cold, oblique, but unequivocal to indicate that he remembered our past acquaintance. His tone succeeded in clearly indicating that the nature of our shared experience would in no way guarantee any special privilege now. It was, I thought, a masterful performance. He invited us to begin.

We had resolved to pull no punches and so laid out a long litany of complaints about endangered academic freedom, censorship, reckless behavior of Islamic students, and finally the pauperizing of professors. He listened carefully. He began to respond by saying that he agreed with almost everything we had said, but added, "as managers of the system, however, we face a multiplicity of problems."

He was interrupted by an assistant informing him that Mr. Khamenei's office was on the line. Khamenei, now the spiritual guide of the Islamic Republic, was in those days the president of the country. Tehran was then, as it is now, rife with rumors about a fierce struggle between the two clerics.

In oppressive societies, rumors are not just surrogate news; they are also tools of subversion. In them, fiction and fact cohabit to undermine any claims of harmony. For instance, in the old regime, people showed their frustration by spreading the rumor that the crown prince was a deaf mute. The poor boy had to be shown on television. Dressed in princely cloth, he muttered a childish sentence to his mother. Under the Islamic Republic, rumor mills turned out periodic stories about the death of Ayatollah Khomeini, and constant tales of inter-clerical divisions.

Rafsanjani began chatting with someone, clearly an assistant of Khamenei. There is, I guess, a universal decorum for phone behavior. Social or political status determines which party comes on line first. Shiite clerics played the game no less seriously than their Western political or business counterparts. After a pause a new conversation began, this time with Khamenei. The tone was cold and businesslike. The subject was Iraqi attacks on Kharg Island that morning. It was the first time Iraqi planes had attacked Iran's most important oil-exporting facilities. Rafsanjani listened more than he talked. Our presence might have made him more cautious and silent.

He only interjected to say that according to the reports he had received, the damages had not been substantial. And he volunteered that, "I think Saddam could only dare do this if he had permission from the two super powers." An interesting way for the managers of the system to think about the world. The telephone exchange ended with Rafsanjani agreeing to attend a late night emergency meeting of the Supreme Defense Council.

Replacing the receiver, Rafsanjani picked up his conversation with us where he had left off, now visibly angry. He said that although he agreed in principle with many of our arguments, we could not hope to be trusted with management of the university. "You don't like us," he said, adding, "We know you would gladly embrace another system if you could." He referred to those professionals who already had chosen a life of exile. He told us that the system's top priority was the war, and that the same zealots who had wrought havoc on the university were the life-line of the war effort and the backbone of the system.

When we left the meeting empty-handed, I thought, There sits a man who has the wisdom to listen, the realism to know what is needed, the pragmatism to say what is appropriate, and the political instincts to remain in power.

While the Revolution had been particularly kind to Rafsanjani, nearly all of the clerics in that block managed to find for themselves some piece of the post-Revolutionary political pie.

Of the secular intellectuals in our cellblock, I know of at least three who were subsequently shot by revolution-ary tribunals. Several others were forced to choose a life of exile. A talented playwright now drives a cab in Paris. A promising director suffers the drudgeries of an émigré life in Los Angeles. The proletarian poet remained in Iran and gave up poetry for a more lucrative profession as a truck driver. So much for the camaraderie of the old prison days, a united front against a common foe. We had failed to realize that the foe was as much inside us as outside.

Prison time moved gruelingly slowly. In memory, that same agonizing time is a fleeting moment. During my months in prison, I was haunted by a sense of despair at the loss of precious moments of my life; in retrospect, that time seems like one of the more fruitful periods of my life. I read Homer's *Odyssey* and understood, better than ever before or since, Ulysses' craving for Ithaca. I read the *Shahnameh* and wondered about the tormented soul of Iran, torn between its Zarathustrian heritage and its Islamic history.

We whiled away some of our time by lecturing one another on topics of our expertise. From a professor of civil engineering, I learned much about earthquakes, while a poet lectured us about Hafez. From the hours and hours of introspection and of listening, observing, and reading, I began to develop a new vision of myself and the society I lived in—a vision at once agonizing and enlightening.

Six Conspiracies
in Search of a Revolution

"Hurry up, they've been calling your name," a friend said.

Fear and anxiety nearly crippled me. Late evening summons were a rarity in Evin and invariably an ominous portent.

A guard waited for me at the gate.

"You called for me?" I inquired meekly .

He asked my name, and assured of my identity, put a blindfold over my eyes and led me by the hand through several corridors and down a couple of staircases. We stopped near a gate. After some inaudible whispers, the door opened. We entered a long, silent hall. Another pause, and shortly another door opened. I was pushed in, my blindfold lifted, and once again, almost a year after the day of my arrest, I found myself in solitary confinement.

"Why have you brought me here?" I asked.

The sound of the key turning in the lock was the only response.

The cell was four steps by six. In the corner stood an unguarded toilet, and a small, partially rusted wash basin. These amenities told me that I would be denied even the "toilet excursions," my only contact with the outside world during my last solitary confinement.

The room's only aperture was a barred and glass window in the ceiling, opening to the roof where armed soldiers, frighteningly contemptuous in their looks, relentlessly marched in their heavy boots.

I spent much of the next thirty hours pacing in my cell. In the morning, at noon, and at around seven in the evening, the door opened long enough for my food ration to be shoved in. Before opening the door, guards commanded me to turn my head away, and look at the blank wall, lest I see their faces and contemplate future revenge. All my inquiries about why I was in solitary confinement received the same silent response.

Past midnight on the second day, I heard someone outside my cell; I faced the wall, the door opened, someone entered and blindfolded me. Again we marched through silent corridors, descended some stairs, and stopped in front of an office door. The guard knocked, and when permission to enter was granted, he lifted my blindfold and gently shoved me into the room.

A heavy-set man, bespectacled and smartly dressed, sat behind a cluttered desk. There was a cot in the corner, neatly made and covered with an Army blanket, and a picture of the shah towering over the head of the interrogator. He began by apologizing for what he called "the inconvenience." We were to have met yesterday, he said, but his schedule had forced a delay. I knew, and he knew that I knew, he was lying. In the sadistic games interrogators invariably play, anxious hours of waiting is their form of foreplay. They want you numb with anxiety by the time you enter their offices.

The interrogator then delivered what was clearly a well-rehearsed and probably often-repeated narrative. He spoke of the imminent glorious birthday of His Imperial Highness Shahanshah Aryamehr. He reminded me of the infinite grace of forgiveness with which His Highness had been endowed. He added that in keeping with an annual custom, a number of political prisoners were to be pardoned on the anniversary of the royal birthday. And then, with a mixture of mirth and menace, he concluded by saying that my name was on the amnesty list, pending some final minor paperwork.

Then he commented on the wonderful opportunities open to an educated man like myself, and pushed a paper in my direction, uncapped his pen, and with all the grace and nonchalance an interrogator can muster, said, "Sign here, and we'll be all done."

It did not take me long to realize what this "minor paperwork" consisted of. With desperation and anger, I said, "I can't sign this. I won't become your informer."

His congenial manner suddenly gave way to a vulgar and threatening tone. He grabbed the letter, crumbled it, threw it in the garbage can, called in the guard, and yelled, "Take this idiot to his cell. Go rot away! Your family was told of your release. They'll be expecting you. If you don't have pity for yourself, pity them." Here he paused, and then added, "Let me know if you change your mind. Without the letter, there is no freedom."

My blindfold was replaced, and soon I found myself back in solitary.

The next four days were a torment. All day I dreamed of the freedom that seemed within my reach, and all night I dreaded the cost of signing that letter. I spent hours conjuring hopeful arguments to keep some optimism, some hope-against-hope while I waited.

On the sixth, with the king's birthday only two days away, I was once again taken to an office. This time, another interrogator awaited me. Much of the last conversation was repeated. Once again I said I would not sign the form.

"But some kind of a letter is mandatory," he replied in a tone of conciliation.

After some bickering, I agreed to write a short note, promising never to engage in subversive acts against the government. The interrogator said he would show the note to his superiors, adding, "I'm not sure they'll accept it."

Soon afterwards, I found myself back in my cell, over-wrought with despair.

The next day, a guard took me to a room where some thirty other blindfolded prisoners waited. Through furtive glances, a staple of all our blindfolded times in prison, I realized that several of those waiting were from cell block Number One, including some of the clerics. This time the guards were clearly less stringent about how tightly we kept our blindfolds on.

An enclosed van took us to the *Komiteh*, where my sojourn had begun. Our belongings, confiscated at the time of arrest, were returned. We were led to a courtyard and just outside the door our blindfolds came off. It was drizzling outside. The gate opened, and with a strange sense of hesitation and exhilaration, I walked to freedom. The Islamic Revolution was a little more than a year away.

But at that moment, an Islamic Revolution seemed absolutely impossible. When the Revolution did come, it brought an avalanche of strange conjectures. The inexplicable lends itself not only to myth making and fantasy, but to conspiracy theories as well. In them, the incomprehensible is tamed into something manageable. The purpose such theories serve in Iranian society is, I think, comparable to the function of astrology in America. It feeds on a kind of paranoia, yet it delivers a soothing sense of certitude.

To go by the common lore of these conspiracy theories in Iran, in the whole of the last century, not a single Iranian of prominence seems to have died of natural causes. With every crack in the edifice of the status quo, a new "fact" was appropriated for the armory of the conspiracy theories that claimed to explain, and even predict, the chaotic contours of the unfolding Revolution. The theories ranged from the banal to more ingenious, though often convoluted, narratives. Equally expansive was the canvas of culprits—from a Zionist-imperialist collusion to an authority no less than the good Lord himself, with a myriad cast of other major or minor forces and figures.

A few weeks before the Revolution, on a crisp, cold wintry night, a friend called my house in Tehran. "Have you seen it?" he inquired, and aghast at my ignorance, urged me to look at the moon. A rumor, unknown in its origins, had spread over the city. A shadow of Ayatollah Khomeini was purported to have appeared on the moon. For the devotees of the exiled messiah, the moon image was a reassuring sign of a cosmic design and intervention. For some of his opponents, it was a cunning British trick.

Even in my earliest childhood recollections, the "hand of the British" was the theme of most political discourse. From the Constitutional Revolution of 1905 to the rise of the Pahlavi dynasty, from the fall of Reza Shah to the rise of Ayatollah Khomeini, every major and many minor events in Iran's political history were said to have been masterminded by the British. A cruder version of this theory was articulated around the time of the Revolution in the form of a joke. "Under every mullah's turban is a sign, Made in England."

In fact, an organic element of the British theory has always been the claim that mullahs historically have been key instruments of English policy in Iran, and this observation is part of a more elaborate analysis of foreign conspiracies in the country.

189

In their colonial endeavors, the British are said to successfully camouflage themselves in the labyrinth of existing social institutions. Knowing how slowly things change in the Middle East, they are cautious about advocating rapid change. Instead, they try to direct existing social movements and institutions into patterns amenable to Her Majesty's interests. Since few institutions in Iran have been as enduring as that of the Shiite clergy, it seems reasonable to the proponents of this theory that the British would be tempted to infiltrate the ranks of the mullahs.

Americans, on the other hand, are said to be dangerously naive and hopelessly optimistic about debunking traditions and erecting modern, American-modeled institutions in their place. According to certain theorists, the British had parlayed their long colonial past into cunning mastery of Iranian politics, while the youthful ignorance of the United States had made her dangerously incompetent. My uncles, active players in Iranian politics, often talked about the complex and competitive relationship between these two governments as an unfair match: "An experienced fox jousting with an inexperienced hen," in their words.

In fact, at least one variety of the existing conspiracy theories has the Islamic Revolution engineered by the

British to subvert and supplant the U.S. position in the Persian Gulf region.

Masonic lodges are believed to be the chief catalysts and coordinators of British policy in Iran. There has developed a whole historical narrative, with its own unique lexicon and logic, that explains modern Iranian history through the prism of Free Masonry. A four-volume book, with a list that included the names of many of Iran's political, intellectual and economic elite, was published some thirty years ago, claiming to represent only a partial list of Iranian Free Masons. (Soon afterwards, another list of Iranian politicians who were allegedly connected with the American government was published. Conspiracy connoisseurs suggested that the two lists were part of a battle between the U.S. and British intelligence forces in Iran.)

When in the early eighties, the author of the book on Free Masons, by then a septuagenarian, died of an apparent heart attack, Masons were suspected of murder, with revenge the prime motive. In the minds of many Iranians, Free Masons are assumed to be Britain's fifth column, a secret brotherhood out to conquer the world, and the scope of their conspiracy is not purely political.

When the Revolution was a few months old, in a cor-

191

ner of the afternoon newspaper, I read about an upcoming lecture entitled "Karl Popper and the Masonic-Zionist secular conspiracy." I knew the speaker, Fardid. He was an erudite professor of philosophy who had written, some forty years ago, a seminal article about the philosopher Heidegger. Like his mentor, Fardid was notorious for his new vocabulary.

The lecture was to be held in a classroom in the Faculty of Arts and Letters. The Islamic Student Association, known as a den of fanatics, was the event's sponsor. In light of rumors of the professor's dalliance with the recently overthrown monarchy, this was, I guess, his penance; his insurance against a disruption of retirement benefits. Revolutions are like relationships. They can bring out the best or the worst in us, and this was surely not one of the professor's finer hours.

The room was inhabited by a few bearded men and fewer veiled women. My shaved face was enough to make me an oddity in the small audience. With a delay that seems to have become customary for almost all events in Iran, the speaker finally arrived. He was a pathetic sight to behold behind a thick pair of glasses that constantly slipped to the end of his nose. Sweating profusely in an oversized shirt buttoned to the top and a baggy suit, he began to speak.

He spoke of a humanist conspiracy masterminded by the Masons, funded by the Zionists, and actualized by Westophile intellectuals. "They are the curse of this nation," he said. "The walls of this academy reek with the poisons of European Enlightenment."

In his long meandering speech, he never even mentioned Popper. With no hint of irony, he used a heavily Heideggerian language to denounce all intellectuals who look to the West for their inspiration and often knowingly become agents of the Masonic-Zionist plot.

The audience seemed impressed yet confused. Failing to understand the flow of his narrative, they clung to an ambiguous aura of insight and justice they attributed to his words. Revolutions are, I think, a coagulation of private agendas with public grievances. They are the instinctive acquiescence of a mob, roused and ravaged by resentment and injustice, to the private agendas of their leaders. In the case of the professor, his private agenda to save his pension coincided with the audience's need to have its belief in Western imperialist conspiracies validated by a Western-educated intellectual.

That day the professor concocted fantastic tales about British intellectual conspiracies in Iran, but there were as many theories about the role of America in Iran—that the U.S. government overthrew the shah in apprehension of Iran's emerging economic prowess was one. "We were becoming a second Japan" is how a historian of some repute articulated the theory, claiming further that at the 1979 Guadeloupe conference of the heads of the seven industrial nations, Carter finally convinced the other leaders that the shah, as the engineer of this new economic miracle, must go.

For some, including the shah himself, the politics of oil fueled and funded the Iranian Revolution. According to this theory, the shah raised the price of oil and the oil companies (or the seven sisters) decided not only to get rid of the king, but to punish him as well. The shah was to be banished, he was to become a pariah. And any world leader who defied America's strictures against helping the shah paid a heavy price. A friend of mine and an avid proponent of this scenario tried to convince me of it by reminding me that the shah spent his exile in Panama and Egypt, and "Sadat was assassinated; Torijo of Panama died a suspicious death; and Noriega, who was then head of security in Panama, is now rotting in a Miami jail!"

Other conspiracy connoisseurs see Carter as an instrument of a larger conspiracy. They say Iran is a piece of a larger puzzle being manipulated by the Trilateral Commission. Proponents of this view claim that the Commission, an offshoot of the Council on Foreign Relations, obviously runs U.S. foreign policy and that sometime in the mid-seventies, they charted a new course. Corrupt authoritarian regimes that stayed in power thanks to U.S. support were to give way to more populist regimes. "Iran was the test case," an advocate of the theory reminded me, "followed by the fall of Pinochet in Chile, Marcos in the Philippines, and Zia in Pakistan."

Then there is the Green Belt theory, green being the color of Islam. The Islamic Revolution, it says, was concocted by Washington to create in Iran, Pakistan, and Afghanistan a viable Islamic alternative to communism. With the grace of the green line, or a series of societies run by Islamic governments, not only the Persian Gulf and the Indian Ocean would be safe from Soviet incursions, but the many millions of Muslims in the Soviet Union could be agitated into a destabilizing movement.

Fascinating as the Masonic and American possibilities were, they paled in comparison to the story of Fardust, the consummate conspirator. The web of intrigues attributed to him is nothing short of mythical. He is our Rasputin, minus the sexual subtext.

195

I had heard of Fardust before the Revolution. He was known as the shah's closest confidant. "The only friend he has," people said. When as a crown prince the shah was dispatched by his father to a Swiss boarding school, Fardust accompanied him. How he was chosen is a mystery. Some say he was the son of the royal gardener. Others think he was placed in the position by one of the European intelligence agencies.

Fardust remained with his royal master through thick and thin. Erotic entanglements were even hinted at. He was a four star general and said to be the shah's liaison with SAVAK. At the same time, in a ruling circle notorious for its conspicuous corruption and consumption, he had the reputation of being one of the very few honest men. He lived modestly and shunned the limelight. His absence from the public arenas of power was part of his enigma and an added source of power. "He's the shah's eyes and ears," my uncle used to say.

I finally saw Fardust on television in the only public address he ever gave—a report on the findings of a Royal Commission on governmental corruption and inefficiency, a belated response to the rising tide of revolution. His contorted face, his fidgety posture, his inability to even read the text of a prepared speech all subverted the aura of power ascribed to him.

Not long afterward, revolutionary fever reached a high pitch and Fardust was temporarily forgotten. In the last days of the old regime, one of his protégés, a General Gharabaghi, was appointed the chairman of the Joint Chiefs of Staff. It was he who, on the morning of the Revolution, declared the armed forces "neutral" and thus facilitated the more or less peaceful transition of power to the new Islamic government. Soon after that, almost all of the pillars of the old regime and the top brass of the royal army could be accounted for. Those most fortunate had fled; many had been executed by firing squads; and the rest, with few notable exceptions, were awaiting trial in prison. Of Fardust there was not a word.

Then the rumors began. The Revolution had been an inside job and Fardust had been the pivotal man. He had deliberately deceived the monarch, subverted social policy, betrayed state secrets, and cold-bloodedly prepared the demise of his master. In *Answer to History*, the shah called Fardust "one of my closest friends," who went on "to betray me. He is now head of SAVAMA, Khomeini's secret service." In a famous television interview with David Frost, tears seemed to spill out of the shah's eyes when he was asked about Fardust. Others said that Fardust had been working for "them" for more than forty years.

For some, "them" was Ayatollah Khomeini and his movement. For others, it referred to the British. Still a third group believed the CIA. was behind "them." But the biggest surprise came from the Islamic regime itself.

One day, some five years after the Revolution, the official newspapers ran a small, seemingly insignificant item. Fardust had been arrested. The decidedly nonchalant tone of the news was a sure sign of serious business. The announcement also indicated that the general's confession that he had been a veteran KGB agent was soon to be broadcast on television.

Only a short episode of what was expected to be a long confession was shown. And then Fardust was never seen or heard from again. The official version had him dead by a heart attack. Conspiracy connoisseurs knew better.

Even after his alleged death, Fardust continues to tantalize the imagination of conspiracy buffs. Early in 1990, a two-volume book was published by an institution that calls itself the Center for Political Research. The Center is generally believed to be a euphemism for the Islamic Republic's secret police. Volume one was titled *The Memoirs of the Ex-Five Star General, Hossein Fardust*. Volume two was a collection of government documents, including the political testimony of an Indian man called Ardeshir Jee.

In comparison to the bizarre world depicted by Fardust's memoirs, all conspiracy theories seem believable. He writes with no sense of remorse of his intimate connection with British intelligence. He depicts a king, his master of forty years, whose every move was dictated by either British or American ambassadors to Iran. He writes of the days immediately after the Allied occupation of Iran in World War II. Reza Shah had been deposed, and every night for about ten days, Fardust traveled to the British Embassy at the behest of his young prince. There, under cover of dark, he would meet an embassy official. The fate of the Iranian monarchy was apparently being decided, and the prince was anxious to know whether His Majesty's government would agree to maintain the monarchy in Iran and agree to his ascension to the Peacock Throne.

Fardust describes whole sections of the vast Iranian intelligence network that reported only to British and American officers. Most baffling of all, he writes of Shapour Jee, an obscure man who was presumably Her British Majesty's unofficial but omnipotent viceroy in Iran.

The core of the second volume of the general's memoirs is the text of the political testimony left by Ardeshir

Jee—Shapour's father, and a consummate king maker, worthy of Warwick himself. Apparently it was Ardeshir who first interviewed an unknown colonel named Reza Khan and recommended him to the British as the suitable candidate to fill the newly vacant post of the Iranian monarch. When Reza Khan was enthroned as the Reza Shah and founded the Pahlavi dynasty, Ardeshir was at his side for every significant political decision and appointment the king made. When Ardeshir died, his powers were transferred to his son. Indeed, if we are to believe Fardust, every political decision made in Iran during the fifty years of Pahlavi rule was made or at least significantly influenced by this little-known Indian father and son.

Foreign powers were not of course the only important conspirators of Iranian politics, as I was reminded when the Revolution was in its fifth year. The reign of terror raged unabated. Fear was endemic. The economy was in shambles. The war with Iraq was escalating and aerial bombings of Tehran had intensified. Tehran was a vanquished city, its nerves taut as a bow, its nights riddled with anxiety and missiles, and its people nearly hopeless.

One gloomy afternoon, when I went to buy some bootleg vodka from a much-appreciated Armenian neighbor, he seemed uncharacteristically jovial. "Have you heard about it?" he asked, and without waiting for my response, invited me into his house. He reached for a Persian translation of the Bible and, opening it to its marked place, said, "It won't be long now; their days are numbered." Then he reminded me of the infallible dreams of Daniel and began a clearly well-rehearsed recital, punctuated by pregnant pauses. He read about Daniel who dreamed of being in the province of Elam, of a ram who pushed his horns against the west and the north and "acted according to his own will and became great." He read about a goat that came from the west, and "when he was come near the ram, he was enraged against him, and struck the ram and broke his horn." My neighbor described the subsequent grandeur of the goat, and the continuous sacrifices the goat demanded of his people, and of his bloody 5,300 days rule.

Finally, triumphantly, he read Gabriel's interpretation of the dream. The ram was none other than the king of Persia and by then I needed no Gabriel to tell me who the goat was. I bought my vodka, hoping that at least this time, the good tidings of the Book were not metaphoric. Like most Iranians, I too had been addicted to metaphoric ambiguity all my life. That night I craved a bit of literal language in heavenly discourse.

―――――――――――― Dreams In Exile ――――――――――

Exile is when you live in one land and dream in another.

Societies, and individual relationships for that matter, are as good as the dreams they foster. In my last years in Iran, when middle-class life was, by force, driven underground and nightly parties became a central fixture of our lives, I often listened to people's dreams and nightmares and thought that they, better than any scholarly essays or political manifestos, could provide the existential flavor of life under a system of revolutionary terror.

Caught up in writing these memories, I had a dream last night. Like almost all my other remembered dreams, I was in my old childhood home, this time in the kitchen. The smoke and soot of many years had blackened the room. On top of the log-burning brick stove sat a big black kettle, something I saw almost every day of my childhood when, returning from school, I looked to see what was being prepared for lunch. The log was burning evenly. But then I felt warm air behind me. I turned to find myself surrounded by logs, all aflame, scattered across the floor. What awoke me was not the fear of the fire but of my inability to escape it. I thought the meaning of my dream quite evident. Looking into one's past might well uncover hidden fires.

I have been interested in the meaning of dreams from childhood, as many in my family are. Later I discovered it to be a social pattern. Dreams were codes, a mortal's only connection with the divine, occasionally soured by the devil's interception. Dreams were premonitions, forays into the world of the dead, a sacred forecast of pending emotional, financial, or physical problems and prospects. The veracity of a dream correlated directly with the piety of the dreamer. An idiom of the Persian vernacular shows the society's deep affinity with the predictive and prescriptive powers of a dream. If someone speaks with certitude about uncertain events, one might, in surprise or even dismay, ask, "What, are you dream-struck?"

Dreams were part of traditional society's legitimizing discourse. Kings and clerics, the two pillars of power in

Persia, both used them profusely to foster and legitimize their claims to divine authority. As late as the early 1960s, a monarch as ostensibly modern as Mohammed Reza Shah wrote in his much publicized memoirs of his divinely inspired dreams.

Like all sign systems, dreams too need decoders. Shiite texts are replete with guides and structures for dream analysis. They claim that a dream's tidings vary with the purity and piety of not only the dreamer but of the interpreter as well. A virtuous analyst will deliver salvation, while dreams interpreted by a sinner can only harvest havoc and misery. The medium is part of the calculus of the message.

My maternal grandmother and my sister's nanny were our family's dream decoders. The pattern of their interpretations was similar, every element of a dream was a sign with predetermined meanings. As a rule, most signs heralded the reverse of what they seem to convey. While water meant happiness, the embrace of the dead brought a long life. Snakes meant prosperity, and weeping signaled joy. The saints were said to be the sole sages of this sacred language. I remember once asking my sister's nanny why God had not designed his codes in a simpler fashion where signs would correspond more directly with what they signified. Surprised and slightly amazed at what must have seemed to her a brazen question of an ill-mannered child, she told me impatiently, "Only He knows the reasons for His actions."

Iranian royal courts often had their own official dream decoders, magis moonlighting as astrologers and dream analysts. In spite of its proximity to power—in Iran always synonymous with power itself—the job was hardly coveted. Many a head rolled when the message was unpleasant or the prediction unrealized.

Not only were there "authorized" decoders in our family, there were also renowned "good dreamers." One such privileged person was Ashraf Sadat. To the great dismay of my father, who despised her as a charlatan, she visited our house often. She was a distant cousin of meager means. My mother believed in the magic of her dreams. The old lady always arrived jubilant about the good tidings of her dream from the previous night. One day it was my maternal grandfather she had seen, a halo around his head, conversing with my mother. Another time she had dreamed of my mother walking through a lush garden, led by a saintly man of whose countenance the dreamer had only caught a glimpse. Every dream was handsomely recompensed. Who, after all, dared ignore the call of the sacred or of the dead?

The more alienated, insecure, and marginalized people feel, the more they turn to divinely coded dreams or other heavenly messages. It was not then surprising that in the tumultuous days of the Revolution, almost the whole multimillion population of the modern metropolis of Tehran poured into streets, backyards, or rooftops and sought and indeed found the shadow of Ayatollah Khomeini on the moon—a dream of divine benediction for what was by then already an irresistible political reality.

A couple of years after that full moon night, I was traveling with a friend to the central parts of Iran. Suddenly, in the midst of the barren desert, just across the city of Qom, Farokh and I came upon an ornate giant mosque, skirted by a throng of people. We stopped. The mood was joyful, the atmosphere one of a carnival. Colorful Persian rugs were spread all around the mosque. Men in pajamas, and women with scarves on their heads and chadors wrapped around their hips bustled about. With steaming samovars everywhere, here were all the necessary elements of a Persian picnic. We finally mustered enough courage to approach the friendliest face in the crowd and ask him about the occasion for the celebration. Dismayed by our ignorance, in a patronizing tone, he told us that when the twelfth Imam returned, he would emerge from the well located in the yard of the mosque. Those congregated wished to be early conscripts in the Savior's army.

Shiite religious texts are replete with accounts of the twelfth Imam's apocalyptic return. One famous source claims that upon his reappearance, rivers of blood, reaching the saddle of his horse, will follow in his wake. The Return will be, another reliable narrative reports, on the day of the Imam's birthday. And that day, we already know, was the birthday of the Mehdi.

We had seen exuberant celebrations everywhere we had been. Every year before the Revolution, the Pahlavi regime had tried to make all businesses and neighborhood committees celebrate the shah's birthday. Out of fear, many complied, but somehow succeeded in showing their ambivalence. In contrast, when the birthday of the Mehdi came around, neighborhoods, particularly in the poorer sections of town, celebrated with as much grandeur as they could muster. Posters arched across the streets, with a message that was ostensibly religious, but was in fact politically subversive. "Happy Birthday to the Only True King" was a particularly popular slogan in those days.

I had even read about small cities and villages that, well into the mid-twentieth century, saddled a horse on every Thursday night and tied it near the entrance to their village—in case the messiah arrived and needed to commence his bloody battle against the infidels, apostates, and sinners.

Having witnessed the jubilation of the crowd waiting in the desert for their savior, Farokh and I drove on. Around dusk, we arrived at a small village near the city of Kashan. We were there to visit the graveside of Sohrab Sepehri, a poet and painter of infinite taste who was to Iranian modern poetry what Eliot is to the English poetry of the twentieth century. Leukemia had killed him two years earlier. He was only fifty-two when he died. He had asked to be buried in the village.

Amidst the mud-huts, there loomed a mosque monumental in size, a green flag fluttering atop its turquoise tiled dome. A martyred descendent of one of the twelve Imams was said to be enshrined in the mosque, one of the several hundred thousand such holy men buried in every corner of Iran.

An ebullient mood filled the light-flooded courtyard. We asked several people about the poet's grave. None had heard of him. Eventually we located the mosque's caretaker.

We offered him a handsome cash token of our appreciation and asked him to lead us to the poet's burial place.

He led us to a dark, desolate courtyard on the right side
of the turquoise dome. In the middle of the yard, he
stopped, gently tapped the earth with one foot, and then
nonchalantly said, "He is here."

My friend and I spent a half hour of uneasy chatter and
contemplation in that desolate place. Eventually, we
returned through the throng of celebrants waiting for the
Messiah and drove on to our next destination.

The dream of a Messiah descending from heaven or
levitating from a well has appeared many times during
the several millennia of Iran's history. The repeated failure of the Messiah to appear or to dispense salvation has
yet to mitigate the need for or the belief in such divine
intervention. In fact, in spite of the many Messiahs turned
monsters, people still avidly look up to the heavens (or
down a well) for redemption from earthly oppression.
And thus it is that a history of oppression has turned
Iranians into exiles in their own land, living on this earth
and dreaming of heavenly Messiahs.

─────────── Shadow On the Moon ───────────

Aboard a flight called Revolution, he was returning home triumphant after fifteen years of exile. Next to him sat a young man, a close confidant, smartly dressed, the smile of victory on his lips. Transfixed by the television, I, along with much of the nation, watched anxiously as a reporter approached His Holiness and asked what he felt at this momentous occasion. The grim look on his bearded face did not change. Oblivious to the gaze of the camera or of the awaiting nation, he said curtly, "Nothing." The year was 1979. Not long afterwards, the young man who had accompanied him, along with thousands of others, was shot by a firing squad.

Thousands waited for him at the airport. Another estimated two million people lined the streets to greet him.

I stayed home. Though I knew history was in the making on the streets, I also felt something menacing in the air. By then, the early euphoria of the unfolding Revolution had been replaced by an ambiguous but sobering, sense of fear.

While in exile for more than a decade, the old man had lived in a simple house a couple of blocks from where he prayed and lectured on theology and the evils of the regime that had exiled him in 1964. A river flowed two blocks away. Not once did he walk those two blocks to see it flow.

When in his youth, he made a pilgrimage—the only voluntary trip he ever took outside Iran—the one novelty he brought back was a transistor radio. Though frighteningly self-referential in his attitudes and obsessed with reading and rereading a few texts as the only source of wisdom and knowledge, he kept that radio as his close companion for the rest of his life. With it he faithfully listened to the news, particularly Persian programs on the BBC, Radio Israel, and the Voice of America. Using the texts to create a self-righteous and unbending inner vision, he needed the news to chart a course in the labyrinth of a reality outside that was becoming increasingly foreign and hostile.

Not much is known about the life of Ayatollah
Khomeini. An orchestrated ambiguity surrounds his past,
and ambiguity is the stuff of which legends and myth are
made. Some claimed he was the incarnate messiah, a
divinely guided architect of the promised millennia.
Others denigrated him as an illiterate demagogue who
lacked moral scruples and was driven by envy and an insatiable lust for power. For some, he personified the courage
of a small nation to stand against the superpowers. Others
saw him as a fanatical anachronism. Even the simple question of the correct transliteration of his name remains
unresolved: Khumanie, Khomeini, Khoumani. . . .

I first heard of him when I was about ten years old. My
mother considered herself a follower of his. In retrospect,
two factors may have contributed to her appreciation for
the defiant cleric. In those days, the shah had begun a
process of land reform as a result of which my parents
were about to lose the two villages they had inherited as
family heirlooms. Furthermore, the king had also recently
dismissed one of my uncles, of the old school of Iranian
politics, from his post. A new breed, usually educated in
the United States, seemed to be on the rise. I often heard
my mother and uncle talk about the Ayatollah's fearless
rebelliousness. The fragments of facts I knew about him

hinted of danger and inspired awe.

Throughout my college years, Ayatollah Khomeini always seemed to be present on the margins of the movement against the shah. As secular activists in the student movement, we adopted a patronizing attitude toward him. Religion was, after all, the opium of the people. Though he trafficked in it, we forgave him on account of his bold posture against the shah.

In 1978, the Ayatollah was suddenly catapulted into the center of Iranian politics. A small anonymous article, referring to him only by allusion, mentioned his Indian rather than Persian lineage. While some of the article's allegations turned out to be fairly accurate, at the time angry riots broke out in protest. The Iranian government panicked. Hoping to stem the tide, the shah encouraged the Iraqi government to expel Ayatollah Khomeini. France agreed to give him temporary asylum, and overnight the nearly reclusive mullah was an international celebrity.

A few weeks before the Revolution, a friend of mine went to Paris to visit him. In those days, Iranians from all walks of life made the Paris pilgrimage. Some went to cut a deal, others to negotiate a price for political penance, and a few, like my friend, to have an audience with a legend. He came back all but entranced. "He is a true mystic, suffused in a sweet spiritual aura," he said of Khomeini.

Another friend, a university professor active in one of the myriad leftist organizations, deftly dismissed that appraisal and with the arrogance and certainty common among revolutionaries, said, "He is nothing but a reactionary mullah; we'll use him like a stick; when we get rid of the monarchy, we'll throw him away too."

For my part, I thought the anachronism of the Ayatollah's ideas would undo him. "This is the twentieth century," I used to say. "Nobody can take his ideas seriously." It did not take us long to realize how wrong we all had been.

Ayatollah Khomeini was a private man with a public agenda. In him hermeticism cohabited with an extreme sense of social activism. He managed to sustain this contradiction through unwavering regimentation. In the individual realm, his affairs, from nocturnal meditations to his daily meals, were rigorously structured by a minutely detailed and punctual pattern. On the social plane, the affairs of politics, inseparably linked with the affairs of theology, were to be regimented by a leader cum shepherd who attended to every detail of the life of the movement and of the masses who participated in it.

In the span of his long life (1902-89), Ayatollah

Khomeini wrote and lectured on a wide variety of theological, political, philosophical, and jurisprudential topics. In them, he emerges as a prolific pundit and a rigorous thinker with a relentless commitment to a theocentric vision. In fact, beneath the apparently sprawling structure of his books, proclamations, speeches, and interviews, there was a fairly consistent core of ideas and dogmas that he articulated carefully throughout his life. He was, in both temperament and theological persuasion, a passionately political man. At the core of his vision was a loathing of secular modernity, an attempt to re-divinize the world and sacramentalize the ordinary. The establishment of a clerical theocracy was, in his opinion, the only way to achieve salvation and social justice. For him, the sacred value of the ends he struggled for legitimized occasional acts of what Shiites call *taghiye*, or expedient dissimulation.

His many interviews in Paris were probably the most notorious cases of such expedient dissimulation. In those days, when talking to reporters, he made many ambiguous but tantalizingly liberal pronouncements. Once in power, he reneged on all his liberal promises. To his diehard followers, those pronouncements were acts of dissimulation and symbols of his political genius. Opponents called them acts of brazen opportunism and hypocrisy.

Ayatollah Khomeini was in no sense a popular writer. Few of his books were widely read. Their reputation was due to the force and notoriety of the movement with which he was associated. Many intellectuals refused to read his books, dismissing them as medieval gibberish. "Why do you waste your time reading them?" one of my friends asked me. Another friend feared that my curiosity about Ayatollah Khomeini's writings was a first step in my political conversion to his cause.

His narrative styles were as varied as the topics on which he expounded. In sermons and talks targeted for mass consumption, his language was that of a prophet. He spoke in the name of universal laws emanating from a heavenly source. Often he did not seek to argue but offered simple absolute truths. The language was judgmental. It bore no sense of introspection; it fostered no ambiguity; it was unequivocal. On the surface it seemed loose and nonchalant, yet one could detect its precision. Infusing his own peculiar, frequently Arabicized lexicon with a provincial "street talk," he forged a populist language devoid of all conceptual contraptions, appealing and apprehensible to the common folk and their common sense. Indeed, the contrast between his style of politics and that of the shah he overthrew is probably

217

nowhere more evident than in their different styles of discourse. The haughty, distant, and often discordant narrative style of the shah smacked of elitism, while Khomeini's vernacular discourse hinted at his populism.

Upon his death, a collection of his mystical poetry, replete with lamentations of love, was published by the government with great fanfare. While he was alive, fawning commentators praised his simple style. When he died, the very same pundits used his mystical poetry to soften his ogre image. On the other hand, many of his foes all but denied his authorship of the poems. Their lyrical descriptions of love and florid praise of wine was incongruent with their image of Khomeini as a political despot and social prude.

On yet another level, when expounding on esoteric subjects of Shiite jurisprudence, Ayatollah Khomeini's language was sober, somber, and lacking individuality, repeating the style of a long tradition of clerical discourse. It was a jargon of authority that claimed divine authenticity. Devoid of all imagery, full of commandments, rigorous and precise, it conjugated every one of its verbs in the imperative.

A prime example of this style can be found in *Clarification of Questions*, easily the Ayatollah's most widely read book. After his exile in the early sixties, it became a banned book in Iran. I first saw it in my mother's hand, who flaunted it not just as a token of her newfound piety, but also of her political bravado. In both structure and substance, the book is similar to a whole array of other *Clarifications* written by other Ayatollahs. Such a book is, in a sense, the rite of passage for becoming a top cleric of Shiism. More specifically, Shiite clerics can use the revered title only if they have published their own version of this kind of book. Such a publication also allows it's author the important privilege of collecting religious tithes.

In the tradition of such practical catechisms, the book contains a whole set of questions and answers covering all facets of life, from modern banking and partnership to precepts on ejaculation and menstruation. The voice that asks these questions is amorphous and anonymous in contrast to the "activist" nature of the voice issuing the answers, a metaphor for the docility Ayatollah Khomeini expected of his followers. They were to accept his divinely originated teaching unequivocally, and at the same time, be activists in debunking all other sources of authority.

Although to an outside observer the detailed and sometimes esoteric nature of many of these precepts might indicate a laughable obsession with minutiae, they are nevertheless troubling manifestations of a key aspect of Ayatollah Khomeini's political philosophy. For him, humans were essentially emulators. The saint and the select (or the Imams and the juris-council) emulate the infinite, infallible wisdom of God. The common stock of humanity emulates what the saint and the select, earthly viceroys of heavenly wisdom, command. For the select, the key to the kingdom of knowledge is piety and purity of heart. For the mortal emulators, the path to salvation is submission. In practical and spiritual matters, Khomeini expected his followers to mold their lives on the preaching of his *Clarifications;* in political and philosophical issues, he advocated reliance only upon the scriptural truth. Human rational faculty, finite and mortal, was for him a paltry match for the infinite, immortal, and unwavering wisdom of God.

He was adept at the art of symbolic politics. He conducted his public audiences in a big barren hall from a high, railed balcony. Out of his inner sanctum he would emerge onto the loft, accompanied by the ritualistic cant of the audience, and descend upon the only chair in the hall. The subdued audience, like the ever-present television camera, gazed up at his Olympian perch. At the end of the audience, again accompanied by the chorus of cants, he returned to his inner world through the mysterious door.

During his reign, he controlled all facets of Iranian politics. In every government institution, real power rested with his unofficial representative. He was, more than anyone else, the embodiment and source of power and the status quo in the Islamic republic. At the same time, he tried to remain aloof from the everyday affairs of the government, often claiming to be nothing more than a simple seminarian.

He seemed to have little respect for his own appointed government officials. On several official occasions, when giving an audience to the top leaders of the Islamic Republic, he met them in a pajama-like garment that is often worn by the clerics under their official robes. Instead of his ceremonial turban, a small skullcap covered his head. On his shoulders rested a folded, checkered linen sheet. He sat on a heavy chair. Those present flocked around him, sitting humbly on the floor, thus graphically mindful of who the shepherd was and where the flock belonged.

I thought the shepherd had rather curious ideas about the life of the flock. My years in America had taught me the values of self-assertion as a cardinal element of individuality and engraved in me a respect for the sanctity of individual corporeal existence and pleasure. For Ayatollah Khomeini, self-denial was a key to salvation, and corporeal existence a dangerous finite realm in which folly and temptation endangered our eternal infinite bliss. Individual existence was in itself meaningless, except as a tool for other-worldly salvation.

For me, the most chilling early manifestation of his disregard for human existence was the Ayatollah's response to criticism about summary trials and executions in the Islamic regime. In a tone bereft of any emotion, he maintained that those executed by revolutionary tribunals were of two kinds. Most were guilty, and thus had met their deserved end. A few might have been innocent, and wrongfully executed. In such cases, God would in recompense send the deceased directly to heaven as a martyr. Such martyrs, the Ayatollah concluded, have much to be grateful for. They receive infinite bliss in return for a shorter life in this mortal coil.

Ayatollah Khomeini's nemesis was secularism. In his view, a world devoid of divinity can only be a world of destitution and despair, and the most pernicious consequence of colonialism had been the attempted secularization of Islamic societies. Islam is politics, he often repeated. He advocated the politics of redemption. To him, revolution was more a matter of salvation than of social reallocation of resources. Once he admonished his people for their concerns over worldly comforts, reminding them that such materialistic leanings only befitted donkeys. Occasionally he turned his criticism to technology, fearing that science would ultimately secularize those who use it. "Let them go all the way to Mars or beyond the Milky Way, they will still be deprived of true happiness," he said.

He even thought that his variety of Islam could solve the problems of the erstwhile Soviet Union. I was still in Iran when he sent a special delegation to meet Gorbachev. Iranian television showed extensive clips of the meeting. Several turbaned mullahs and a darkly veiled woman stood on one side, and Gorbachev and his coterie of Communist bureaucrats gathered on the other side of one of Kremlin's more opulent reception rooms. In deference to the sacred words of the cleric, the delegation insisted on delivering his message in Persian. Gorbachev had agreed to listen.

In the message, the Ayatollah predicted the collapse of the Soviet Union. He berated Soviet leaders for pursuing a false materialistic ideology. The solution, he suggested, was in Islam. In fact, Iran would be glad to train a team of Soviet experts in the infinite wisdom of Islamic teachings. Gorbachev listened politely, but never sent the team. There was something at once embarrassing, frightening, and comical about the whole affair.

It was simple and comforting to dismiss the Ayatollah as an aberration, or to blame foreign conspiracies for his rise to power. For me, he became a mirror in which I could see my ignorance of our past and some important aspects of the society I was born into.

Ayatollah Khomeini was not the only enemy of individualism and self-assertion in Iranian history and society. Iran's past was dominated by forces that discourage individualization. As a child, of all the stigmas one could suffer, few were as biting as being called *por-ru*, literally meaning "someone with too much of a face." Parents, teachers, rulers, and preachers all dreaded self-assertion in children, and praised and expected quiet submissiveness.

Writing a memoir is no doubt an act of self-assertion, an explicit recognition of the perceived value of an individual life. Memoirs are all but absent from the rich Iranian literary legacy. It is only in the last two decades that they have become common as a genre. In fact, when talking to Persian friends, I still refer to this narrative as a collection of essays about modernity. I beat around the bush. The word "memoir" makes me uncomfortable. With American friends, my discomfort dissipates.

Even on the question of suffering, I have come to the sad recognition that the essence of Iranian history was much closer to Ayatollah Khomeini's narrative than anything I had imagined. In Iranian culture the problem of suffering has been symbolized mostly in the figures of the ever-present martyr, Hossein (the third Shiite Imam), and the ever-absent messiah, Mahdi (the twelfth Imam), who has been in hiding for more than a millennium and will one day return to end suffering and deliver salvation and justice. It was no accident that millions of Iranians sought the shadow of the messiah on the moon, and that Ayatollah Khomeini called his movement "Hosseini" (or the "Followers of Hossein"). I was not surprised to hear some of the leaders of the Islamic Republic claim that the Ayatollah was indeed the missing messiah, nor did it seem incredible that Khomieni's valet declared after his master's death that on many nights at around four in the morning a strange light suffused in a sacred aura emanated from the Ayatollah's room.

If Ayatollah Khomeini's retort to the question of the reporter on the plane was a metaphor for the Ayatollah's emotional detachment and self-indulgence, the frenzy of the milling crowd at his funeral symbolized the passions he fueled among his followers. He invited boundless devotion from his disciples, yet showed no attachment to any of them. Maybe the muse of history will remember public men for the kind of sentiments they helped awaken in their followers. If so, the image of young boys running to their deaths over a mine field and a frenzied flagellating mob desperately seeking a piece of a shroud as a sacramental relic will shape the legacy of Ayatollah Khomeini.

─────────── Benighted City ───────────

I was in America when Khomeini died. I saw images of his funeral on television. What frightened me wasn't just the sight of waves of frenzied mourners. Equally frightful was the thought that Western observers would misunderstand its meaning and translate it as confirmation of their already negative opinion of Persians.

Revolutions are cauldrons of bewitching images that create the illusion of amity between a powerful ruler and an enthusiastic but otherwise docile and amorphous mass. With their insatiable passion for the carnival, revolutions seem tailor-made for television. For me, the funeral of the Ayatollah embodied all the complexities of this dangerous combination.

Before coming to power, Ayatollah Khomeini had succeeded in forging and holding a united front against the shah by promoting revolution as a panacea for social ills. To the middle classes, it promised political freedom; to the poor it offered a "new deal"—houses with no rents, utilities free of charge. To devout Muslims, it hinted at a pure Islamic regime, a return to a pristine prophetic past. Even the radical left was tantalized by the revolution's anti-imperialist jargon, while imperialists liked its offer of a secure and cheap flow of oil. At the same time, to the Soviet government it suggested curtailed Western influence in Iran. The agenda was clearly inherently contradictory, but in the days before the Revolution, any attempt to discuss these contradictions was tantamount to counter-revolutionary sabotage.

On the eve of the Revolution I wandered aimlessly around Tehran University, browsing in bookstores and rummaging through once illegal books, now piled on sidewalks, hawked by political peddlers. The streets were cluttered with groups of people, each engaged in some passionate political debate. The novelty of freedom had attracted to these gatherings faces that betrayed long years of undernourishment in ideas, faces awed by the civility and decorum of democratic debate. Political chatter, abstract and incomprehensible as it might have been, seemed to flush the faces with a sense of entitlement.

The night before, Muslim zealots had disrupted the lecture of a secular intellectual. The bold headline of the newspaper that day repeated the words of Ayatollah Khomeini, all ideological persuasions will be tolerated in future Iran.

Long before coming to power, the Ayatollah already talked like a head of state. The most significant part of what he had said, however, indicated that ideologies would be tolerated so long as they did not oppose Islam, and this appeared only in small print. Revolutionary movements seem to thrive on a fair dose of delusion and deceit. The Islamic Revolution was not going to be an exception.

I joined one of the gatherings on the sidewalk where two young men were the principal debaters, with sporadic interventions by a few others and the now silent, now animated observation of the rest. They were talking about freedom. One of the two men demanded a more precise definition of Islamic freedom. He criticized the previous night's disturbance. The other young man was calm, bearded, the aura of victory already around him. He insisted that "at this moment, when the Revolution has not yet succeeded," such issues were diversionary. "Only Imperialists want us to squabble amongst ourselves now," he said, deferring all such "diversionary debates" to after the Revolution. But once enthroned, the Revolution left little room for debate.

Language is a source of problems for all revolutions. The structure of language, its ability to conjure memories of the past, interfere with the leveling goal of revolution. Revolutions invariably strive to erase memory. Memory, after all, defies the fiction of a totally new beginning. And so the Islamic Republic encouraged a new Arabicized lexicon. Everyday speech became a political act.

Under the Islamic Republic, I and thousands of others had to decide each day how we would begin our lectures at the university. The new Islamic masters ordained that all lectures begin with an Arabic prayer for the Lord. Because I refused to do this, I began every class session with a great deal of anxiety. I suspect the agonies that come with this kind of choice can only be understood by someone who has lived under a system with a similar compulsion to politicize every facet of life.

Revolutions are also about silence. Through a coercive reign of terror, the Islamic Republic had, unwittingly, enriched our language of silence and our society's lexicon of gestures. Literary language became more metaphoric and the language of gestures became textured with new layers. Glances, brow movements, intonations, body language became pregnant with new precise meanings and possibilities. The faces, the crowd, the gestures of Khomeini's frenzied burial can, I think, only be understood in light of this new vocabulary.

Not everyone on the street on the day of the funeral was a supporter of the Revolution. Hero worship was no doubt a galvanizing force. Ayatollah Khomeini was a cult hero long before enshrining himself as the Supreme Leader of all the Pious in the World. His defiant tone against powerful adversaries, his uncompromising posture, his folksy language, and humble lifestyle had endeared him to many of the dispossessed. It seemed the messiah they had long sought had finally arrived.

Ayatollah Khomeini understood the power of his following. When the hardship of post-revolutionary life began to erode his popularity, he tried to distance himself from the regime he had created. The tone of his pronouncements began to sound more like that of a leader of the opposition than of the Supreme Guide of the Revolution.

I remember a conversation I had with a window washer named Javad who had come to wash the windows of our home. He lived with his five children in a single room.

He spoke of his two teenage sons at the front, fighting the Iraqis. He complained about the injustices of the rationing system, about rising costs of living, and the shortage of medicine. "I walked for five hours to find some penicillin for my daughter," he said. "And when I found it, it was some of this imported Indian stuff. They're no good, you know."

I didn't know. I bought any medicine I needed from the black market, and there, for the right price, any brand was available. I finally mustered enough courage to ask him, "Who do you think is responsible for the shortages?"

"People around the Imam," he snapped. "People who run the government."

My next question, "What about the Imam himself?" seemed to touch a raw nerve in him. He ranted that the Imam was on the side of the poor, that he was surrounded by corrupt officials. "They lie to him all the time. What can he do? He's just one man." The man's need to believe in his messiah, unsullied by worldly incompetence, outweighed any rational argument I could make. Watching the funeral, I knew that Javad would be among the mourners, despairing the loss of his one hope for earthly salvation.

This messianism is a central element of Shiite faith.

The rank of the mourners that day had to be filled with the faithful. But not every devoted Shiite was a supporter of the Revolution, nor was every mourner in that procession there to register support for the dead leader.

There is a belief, popular amongst the Shiites, that blessed are those who mourn the dead and that God offers many a grace to those who attend a funeral and weep for the dead. I first heard this from Ameh, my wife's aunt and as dear to me as my own grandmother, after a neighbor she did not much like had died. She attended the memorial service and returned with red eyes. To my surprised inquiry, she explained, "weeping at any funeral lightens your sin in the day of reckoning."

Ameh was a devout Muslim and a fervent opponent of the Islamic regime. Her magnanimous soul was crammed into a diminutive, yet robust, septuagenarian body. Her life had been an odyssey of suffering, yet her response was a benevolence of mythic proportions.

She had been married off to her cousin at age fifteen, because "my father wished it that way." After a painful year at the house of her critical in-laws, the groom left to find work, never to return. Ameh remained waiting for the rest of her life. "God wanted it that way," she often said. Docile in the face of what she deemed were God's

233

desires, Ameh was defiant and resolute in what she considered human injustices.

She was from Azerbaijan. Though she had lived in Tehran for nearly fifty years, she never spoke a word of Persian. Even to those, like myself, who knew no Turkish, she refused to speak Persian. All through their history, linguistic resistance has been a constant trait of Azerbaijanis in Iran.

Like most of her fellow Turks, Ameh was a follower of Ayatollah Shariatmadari. When the Islamic Republic first charged the old cleric with complicity in an attempted coup, then humiliated him into public repentance on national television, and finally put him under house arrest, Ameh became a resolute foe of the Revolution. Like Ayatollah Shariatmadari, she had been, from the very beginning, skeptical of Ayatollah Khomeini. For her, religion belonged only to the realm of the spiritual needs of the human community, and she believed that the profanities of power would only encroach upon its sanctity.

When the war came and rationing was imposed, Ameh became angrier. Rationing, in fact, radically changed her life. It entailed long waits in lines, and much of that time was spent exchanging political gossip—in this sense, rationing was a double edged sword for the regime.

By the time the war finally reached Tehran, Ameh had learned to accept food shortages; she had grown accustomed to streets bereft of young faces, and to the gradual increase of those with damaged limbs, often on crutches, haunting the crowded avenues. But when the first Iraqi rockets hit Tehran, Ameh changed. There was now more despair in her voice, more prayers for a quick end to her own life. "What's the use?" she often said. "We are like sheep at the mercy of two wolves. The sooner it ends, the better it is."

Ameh was not the only one changed by the war. The whole fabric of the city changed. A sense of dread became a fact of life. Rocket attacks were a permanent fixture of our lives. My young son's paintings grew grimmer by the day. Every house he drew was a target of menacing bombs that floated in the air.

He was five years old then. He and I were the only men in a house inhabited by Fereshteh, her mother, who was living with us while she supervised the construction of an apartment complex she had been saving for all her life, and Hamid's nurse. Ameh was also a regular visitor. The presence of so many women meant an end of privacy for me, but the compensation, a rich life of affection and storytelling and game playing for Hamid, made it more than tolerable. Indeed, my life with Fereshteh had by then reached the stage where privacy is what you dread, not crave. Spending time with Hamid, and working on the many translating and writing projects I had undertaken were my only solace in an otherwise bleak world. It was in those days that I wrote a deeply melancholic book in Persian called *Andre Malraux and the Tragic Vision*, a lengthy commentary on the writings of Malraux from the perspective of the Pascalian tragic vision; a lamentation for the contingency of life and the dread of death. Seeing the bomb-strewn landscape of my son's paintings broke my heart every time.

I even learned that it was possible to achieve a kind of half-sleep through the night. Numbed by anxiety, half the mind slumbers on, while fear keeps the other half tuned to the warning of catastrophe, all but oblivious to other sounds.

The warning was a screaming siren. Then there were seven minutes until the first explosion. To escape the agony of these nights, every evening before dark two to three million people crammed themselves and their valuables into their cars, left the city, and waited until dawn in some remote corner of a road. In the morning they returned to their homes and their routines.

The sight of the exodus every evening only added to
the despair of those like me and my family who stayed in
the city, hoping that it would not be our home hit by Iraqi
rockets that night.

Rumors only compounded our sense of despair. Almost
every night, my friends called me, intending no malice,
to say, "tonight will be different." A carpet bombing of
the city was imminent, they warned. Other times "knowl-
edgeable sources" had informed my concerned callers. I
never understood the dynamics of such implicitly threatening phone calls.

In our house, the only change we made in our routine
was to have Hamid sleep with us in our bed every night.
When the sirens began, my wife and I would sit up in bed,
our often still sleeping son between us, our hands clumsily attempting to shield his ears from the sound. I could
hear my own heart beating; my hands would sweat; my
mouth puckered with fear and anger. Not only I, but a
whole city waited to see whose turn had come that night.

Moments after each raid, the city bustled into action.
Phones began to ring, with rumors about damages, assur-
ances about the safety of loved ones. And then, literally
in a matter of moments, thousands would converge on
the scene of destruction, some to watch, many to mourn,

others to vent anger.

Revolutionary Guards around the scene of the nightly bombings were uncharacteristically tolerant. With reckless abandon, spectators attacked the regime, even Ayatollah Khomeini himself, and the Guards stood by complacently. In fact, in spite of the common notion about the blind terror unleashed by the Islamic Regime, it always seemed to me that they have been masterly Machiavellian in their dispensation of violence. For instance, in the second year of the Revolution, when radical groups in many major cities staged an armed uprising against the regime, the evening news featured an announcer reading reams of names belonging to those executed by revolutionary tribunals during the preceding twenty-four hours. The government also published names of repentant prisoners who, as a token of their repentance, had complied with the demand to execute their comrades of yesterday. And the same regime, on the nights of aerial bombings, allowed people to vent their anger openly against the powers that be.

But as the next day wore on, and a morose and melancholic city haphazardly resumed its routines of the day, the level of the regime's tolerance gradually diminished.

Ameh, oblivious to such nuances, was consistent in her

protestations. "He is the false messiah," she often said. Every time she limped home after a long wait in a line to buy provisions, she complained, "This is God's revenge for our ingratitude." I never found out what she thought she had been ungrateful for, but I do know that, faith-driven as she was, she probably took to the streets the day the Ayatollah died.

Not all the faithful were like Ameh. Some of the most honest supporters of the Revolution came from the ranks of those who saw in Islam a viable agenda for both salvation and revolution. Ali was one of them.

I first met him after a tense lecture I gave in one of my classes at the Law School. The course was political psychology and the subject was Jung. In my biographical introduction, I referred to a book I had just read about a tragic romance between Jung and one of his patients. A bearded young man, whom I knew to be one of the activists of the Islamic Student Association, raised his hand. When I called on him, he began to deliver a stern sermon chastising me for talking about "un-Islamic afflictions like adultery." I responded with a dissertation on academic freedom, and he quoted Ayatollah Khomeini. "We must be vigilant against corrupt Westernized intellectuals."

After class I was in my office, exhausted, frustrated, and humiliated, when there was a soft knock on the door. Ali entered. He had a sparse stubble on his face and wore the khaki gray shirt that was the unofficial uniform of the devout. He introduced himself and apologized for "the inexperience" of the vigilante student. Then the conversation drifted to his classes, to books he had read and to his few months in prison under the old regime. "I was sixteen when I went in," he said.

We met often. His civility, his compassion, his desire for knowledge, his openness to new ideas made his unshakable belief in the Revolution less of a problem in our discussions. For me, he personified the sublime humanism that is often one of the sources of revolutionary movements, and that is almost invariably eclipsed, if not consumed, by the profane expediencies of power.

Then the war came, and Ali disappeared.

A couple of years later, with the same timid knock on the door, he entered my office again. He walked with crutches. His left pants leg was rolled up to the calf. "We needed volunteers to clear a mine field," he said. There had been more volunteers than were needed and the commander chose those who would go. "But the moon was out. We waited three nights for a patch of cloud." He

240

described the mystical union he felt that night with the other volunteers, "the Brothers" he called them. Tears rolled down my face. Whether I was lamenting his abused innocence or my own despair I do not know.

If Ali was compassionate, selfless and idealistic, Habibi was the opposite. His large head seemed to fit clumsily in the oversized, buttoned-up collar of his shirt. He had a peculiar walk—his arms, all the way to the elbows, seemed to stick to his torso. He walked like a robot.

He was our new dean, come to "clean up" the Faculty of Law. Our school had by then developed a reputation as a hotbed of political opposition to the new regime. Nearly forty of the forty-five members of the faculty, including myself, had signed petitions against the use of torture in Iranian prisons and the adoption of a new criminal code based on Islamic rules of retribution.

There was also a historical score to be settled. Traditionally, Iran's courts and legal system had been the monopoly of the clerics. In the thirties, Reza Shah decided to secularize the judiciary and place it in the hands of jurists trained at the Law School. The clerics saw this as a challenge to their authority. The Law School had become the metaphor of that challenge.

Habibi wreaked havoc on the campus. Students, faculty, and staff were subjected to destructive purges. Of nearly 1,400 law students in our school, only 800 survived Habibi's secretive committee. The rest were dismissed.

Soon after his arrival, Habibi convened a meeting of the faculty. He arrived late, intentionally I think. Yet, even before his entrance, signs of change were quite evident. Faculty meetings were held in an old wood-paneled room, hung with portraits of past deans. Some had been judicial and literary luminaries; others had used the school to launch powerful political careers and had become ministers under the old regime. The last time I had been in that conference hall the pictures were hardly visible, paled to a moribund yellow by age, almost the same color as the pale paneled walls. Now, in place of the pictures glared clear rectangular spaces. Habibi knew the dangers of memory.

He sauntered into the room, took a chair at the head of the table and opened his remarks with a Koranic verse. Then he began to speak. He talked of an infection that had permeated the body of the university. The infection was interchangeably called Westophile, decadent, monarchist, Marxist, atheist, heretic, and liberal. When he uttered these concepts, his tone and gestures conveyed that he found the very words contaminated. Then he spoke of the martyrs of the Revolution, of the blood they had shed to create an Islamic society, and of his resolve to turn the Faculty of Law into an institution befitting the Revolution.

Habibi went on to become a powerful member of the House of Representatives, and although I hear that today he is under indictment for graft and corruption, he delivered on his promise to pulverize the Faculty of Law. Not long after that threatening sermon, I and thirty-five other members of the faculty were summarily dismissed from our positions. For a few, the dismissal proved permanent. The rest of us were called back after about a year.

I spent the interim year translating Kolakowksi's three-volume critical history of Marxism. I worked with the kind of feverish tempo that is usually a sure sign of serious emotional stress. The translation, and spending time with my son, were my only sources of happiness in those days. The translation paid for part of my expenses—the rest came, every month, from my father. It provided escape from the torments of my private life as well. My marriage was falling apart. My attempts to keep our marital troubles away from my son and family and our friends—for many of whom we had been the "ideal couple"—only complicated my life. I was having a particularly complicated midlife crisis. I was in my mid-thirties; I had lost all of my utopian illusions; I had lost my job and was dependent on my father for my livelihood; the Revolution had turned into a nightmare; and my love for my wife, for many years one of the mainstays of my life, was waning. My mother remained bedridden and my daily visit to their house, the sight of her sick body and my father's heroic efforts to make her life more tolerable added to my agonies. The only source of light was Hamid and it was only because of him that in those days the temptations of self-slaughter seemed less desirable.

My return to the Faculty of Law was little help. I was told I could only teach graduate students, but there were no graduate students at the school at the time. By then, I had begun translating *The Master and Margarita*. Our nights were marked by fear of Iraqi air attacks and my days were shadowed by the knowledge that varieties of police were investigating every corner of my life.

The one common characteristic of twentieth-century revolutions is that nothing about the private lives of the population is private. Not only had my life become an open book, but unacceptable deeds had become more than social transgressions. They were sinful rebellion against the government of God on earth. That is why one of the first paper banners Habibi installed on the walls of our school carried Ayatollah Khomeini's words indicating that spying for the Islamic Republic is not spying. Those who fight the Islamic regime, he said, are fighting God.

Fear and suspicion became endemic. Innocent but desperate people reported on their peers. Laughter was declared frivolous. Chatter between men and women in the halls was a sin. Several students were expelled from the Law School when they were caught talking to a member of the opposite sex. Existing patterns of social life were smashed and new patterns constructed that were supposedly free from the temptations of sin. A new dress code was enforced. A battery of zealots stood at the school door to make sure that no man in short sleeves, tight jeans, an unbuttoned shirt, or with long hair entered the building.

For women there were cosmetic and veiling cops. I heard of one encounter with them from Farideh, an outstanding student whom I came upon one day, sobbing in the hall. She wore a blue, shoulder-length scarf, a baggy gray knee-high tunic, loose dark pants and flat dark shoes—compulsory uniform for all students. She had a round cherubic face and a normally rosy complexion, but when I found her in the hall that day her face was crimson.

I invited her into my office. She had been called out by

the cosmetic cops and warned against the use of blush. She had assured them that the pink on her cheek was natural. An older woman had angrily scrubbed her face with a wet napkin. When they found no sign of cosmetics, instead of offering apologies the woman had ordered Farideh to cover more of her face. "Pink faces don't become the Islamic Republic," she had said.

Choking on tears, Farideh told me that she had resolved to leave Iran after the end of the semester. I left that summer too. I don't know whether Farideh did. Had she had stayed at the Law School, her brush with the cosmetic cop probably meant that in order to placate the Islamic zealots at the school, and avoid expulsion, she would have made sure that somebody from the school saw her at Khomeini's funeral procession.

Yet another species of participant in that procession were those who had mastered the art of political camouflage, who feigned faith for financial gains. Majid was one such actor.

I met him a couple of years before the Revolution. Like me, he had been an opponent of the old regime. We had a beer together. When Majid was ready for a second round, he turned around, located the old waiter with eagle-like efficiency, and with the demeanor of a colonial slave driver, snapped his fingers and said, "Hey boy, come here." I was shocked and embarrassed by his behavior. Not long afterwards we left the restaurant for Majid's house.

His room had all the trappings of what a marginalized intellectual's abode needed to have in those days: books, some neatly stacked, others dispersed throughout the room, prints of modern masterpieces on the wall, papers in piles on the floor and table, Spartan furniture. Emboldened by the wine he served us, I asked him about his discourteous behavior toward the old waiter. In a distinctly patronizing tone, he said, "we have to confuse the enemy. We have to behave like the bourgeoisie."

When I saw him again after the Revolution, he was a tycoon in a new house with pretensions to Xanadu. It was granite and grand and seemed terribly inhospitable. Koranic verses, inscribed on beautiful blue tile, adorned the entranceway. In spite of his leftist affiliations of the past, his marriage into a family considered a pillar of the old regime, and his own family's faith in the Bahai religion, Majid had played the game, and he knew the rules.

He wore a beard now and often attended the neighborhood mosque. He had landed a managerial position in a big factory confiscated by the government. By siphoning off products for the black market, he amassed a small fortune. With that fortune and his political connections, he bought, at almost no cost, a couple of other state-run enterprises that were being turned over to the private sector.

In that cold granite mansion, Majid's conversation was still replete with words and concepts from his radical days. He even told me of his generous contribution to a publishing house that, in his words, was "committed to progressive works."

Yet, in spite of his jargon, his penance, and his elaborate self-righteous arguments about the need to work within the system to destroy it—the "termite theory," as he called it—he and his type were sure to have been in the streets of Tehran when Ayatollah Khomeini died. Participation was a requisite part of the role they had chosen. I can imagine him saying later that he had gone to observe the theater, to witness history, to watch the frenzy first hand, but I would see his nervous tic, his chain smoking, his shifty, tired eyes, and I would know differently.

Paradise Redux

Woe unto him who has no home

NIETZSCHE

Hamid and Fereshteh joined me a year after my departure from Iran. By the time they arrived, I had a teaching job and felt ready to provide for them. Life in Tehran had become even more intolerable than when I lived there. Iraqi forces had begun to attack the city during all hours of the day. Our reunion was not just a way of getting our son out of the hellish war, but also an attempt to salvage our marriage.

The landscape of Hamid's paintings changed in America. There was more color and fewer bombs and less menace in them. One of his earlier drawings here, full of light and gaiety, now hangs in my office. It also did not take long to recognize that our marriage could not be saved. The love that was required for healing the wounds of our relationship was simply not there.

In the first week of the year 1988, Fereshteh and I separated. Wanting an arrangement that would minimize the
pain of our separation for Hamid, we agreed on joint and
equal custody of our son. I would stay in our rented
house, across the street from where he was enrolled in the
second grade and was learning the English language with
incredible ease. Three days a week, I left the house for a
few hours in the afternoon and Fereshteh came over to
be with Hamid. Then she went back to her own house.
It was under these circumstances that I met Barbara.

It was love at first sight. Her eyes were deep blue and
melancholic, her face chiseled to near perfection, and she
dressed immaculately. Her voice was as tantalizing as her
looks. We talked of a film we had seen. We needed to dis-
entangle ourselves from the lives we had been living. "We
must dispossess before we can possess," she wrote on the
back of a book she gave me then.

Her life was only slightly less complicated than mine.
She had two college-age sons from her first marriage and
when we met she was at the end of a long-term relationship with a man she had once loved, and who still loved her.

We saw each other often, sometimes every day. To me
nothing about her was insignificant. Every move, every
gesture, every color of her dress and every word she said
were signs, now menacing, now mirthful. We shared a

secret language of love.

All my life I had dreamed of such a relationship. But relationships, like individuals, do not exist in a vacuum. First there was the problem of her parents. Though eminently liberal, well-read, and congenial, they counseled against any involvement with an Iranian professor. "Persians have a bad reputation," they had said. "Look at the way they treat women." When reassured that I was a loving and respectful man, their response was unanswerable: "Of course, they're always like that in the beginning. He'll change." Besides, there would be the inevitable elopement with a student in the middle years.

Her parents were not the only problem. Her German friend also warned Barbara about Arabs, and when reminded that Iranians are not Arabs, had dismissed the distinction, "I know, I know, but they're all from the same part." Some of my friends and relatives were no less prejudiced. I remember a dinner conversation she had with one of my brothers, in which he had said, without thinking, "I could never fall in love with an American woman. I don't think any Persian can. She would never share my past, my language, my music." How a benign conversation can become a mine field of emotions!

Language was, of course, a problem. When Persians are together, they invariably speak Persian. In exile, I

think, speaking your native tongue becomes a momen-
tary escape from the constant feeling of disenfranchise-
ment. It is a gesture of communion, of solidarity. It is an
act of defiance, with elegiac qualities. But the experience
is almost never free from tension. Even to the sympa-
thetic outsider, it can, and often does, become a nuisance.

One night Barbara and I had dinner with a Persian
friend, Parviz, and Ruth, his wife of twenty-five years. It
was Barbara's birthday but we had spent the whole day
writing a letter to the *Los Angeles Times* appealing for help
for the victims of the recent earthquake in Iran.
Americans had all but refused to help the Iranian victims,
and I was hoping for a change of heart. I wrote about the
plight of the Iranian people and of the double-jeopardy
and paradox in which they found themselves. They were
ruled by an oppressive regime and now, in times of a natural disaster, Americans denied them help on account of
that very regime.

Attempting to explain this paradox, Barbara said: "Part
of the problem is that you Persians stay together all the
time. You don't consider yourselves part of this society,
you never settle down. You always speak Persian. People
resent that." Her observations were correct, but unfor-
tunately our linguistic problems were not limited to the
occasional Persian I spoke.

If cultures can be said to have geists, then language may be the window to that spirit. Persian is not only the language of poetry, but contains a long litany of potential violations of propriety. Its affinity for metaphor and ambiguity complements the Persian habit of circuitous discourse. There is, invariably, a labyrinth to travel before one can get to the "word within the word." It is a language of many subtle nuances, almost all related to an elaborate system of honorifics. Brevity, particularly in women and children, is prized. The language is rich in metaphor, and in most areas abhors candor. Familiarity is considered an affront. Incredible as it may seem, after two years, and in spite of their constant encouragement, I could never bring myself to call Barbara's parents by their first names.

Barbara was uncommonly eloquent and straightforward in her speech. Talking with her was, for me, one of the pleasures of our relationship. But to my surprise, not all my friends and relatives shared my delight.

I remember our first trip to Los Angeles where I introduced Barbara to my family for the first time. Filled with anxiety, we settled into small talk with the help of a few chilled shots of vodka, accompanied by the customary salted slices of lightly lemoned tomatoes and cucumbers. Into the benign drift of the conversation, she remarked, in that naked style of hers, how good our sex life had been. I could see the discomfort flush my brother's face. But the same decorum that denied such open talk about sex also prevented my brother from articulating his dismay. In Iranian literature erotica has found its niche only in satire; in the vernacular, the vulgar combines with the comic and a whole arsenal of double-entendres. Hassan poured us a new round of vodkas.

The vodka was a relief. Not only was I painfully aware of my brother's reaction, but, with all the protective instincts of a lover, I wanted nothing to blemish my beloved's image. And although her disclosure was music to my ears, my prudish past weighed on me, too. In a way, I think Persian language shares something with Persian domestic architecture where houses are as much places of concealment as comfort. Their public facades are heavily ornamented, while their private amenities are invariably inadequate. In my parent's home the most beautiful rug, the most exquisite antiques, and even the most efficient wall heater (an imported Coleman) all furnished the room set aside for and only rarely visited by guests. In contrast, when Barbara remodeled her house, she put the most elaborate care into the design of her bath.

Aside from these subtle cultural differences, other tensions bore down on our relationship. There had been a time, not long ago, when the Orient was alluring and romantic in America. When I taught Persian at Berkeley in late sixties, many students were smitten with Persia or Persians. One was even preparing to embark upon an opium pilgrimage to Iran and Afghanistan.

But now we were in the nineties and the Oriental lure had been replaced by scraggly bearded, clench-fisted zealots, delirious in anti-American chants, parading blindfolded diplomats around the occupied compounds of the once opulent American embassy. To be in the company of a Persian now was nothing short of valiant. How often I saw the clumsily concealed grimaces on the faces of Barbara's friends when they learned my nationality. How sad I felt when she, in an attempt to absolve me, interjected some disclaimer to distance me from the evils of the Islamic regime and remind her friends of my good qualities. Sometimes my being a minor polyglot helped. On other occasions, my time in prison was my badge of honor. Having had a nanny was always good, for few things seem to impress Americans as much as affluence. I think these are all part of the price of living in exile, particularly as a member of a stigmatized community. But there are other prices as well.

Exile is when you don't read the obituaries, for your dead die elsewhere. How religiously she read them, every day.

255

It was a late night phone call that told me of my mother's death, alone in a hospital. She had been ill for thirteen years. Though she was frail and immobilized by multiple strokes, she had her full wits to the end. On the night before her death, when my father grabbed his jacket to leave, she had asked him to sit for a few more minutes. She had reached for his hands, as my father weepingly recounted on the phone, and said, "Why did it have to end like this?" She reminisced about forty-seven years of "a good marriage." She remembered their first meeting, reminding him of his late arrival at their wedding.

Not long after my father left, she had asked the nurse to bathe her. Clean and freshly robed, she went to sleep, never to wake again.

My family held a wake for her in Los Angeles, where at the time my sister and my three brothers lived. In fact it had been almost twenty-five years—when my older brother left Tehran for medical school in Paris—since the five of us had been in the same place at the same time. Ironically, it took my mother's death to bring it about. Barbara and I drove to Los Angeles for the occasion.

It was a traditional Iranian wake, at once somber and cathartic. It began about two in the afternoon and lasted till about eleven at night. Mournful Koranic recital could be heard the whole time. Only tea and coffee, along with fresh fruits and Persian *halva*, made of flour, butter, and saffron, was served. The more intimate friends and family stayed for dinner.

On our drive back, we talked about the similarities and differences in the way cultures mourn their dead. Barbara told me of her frustration during the wake where everyone had talked in Persian and few had attempted to include her in the ongoing rituals. She talked about the problems of living and planning a life with someone caught in the transience of exile. I understood and empathized with her frustration.

I did feel a kind of transience, and much more then than when I lived here as a college student and my life was consciously transitional, a life of suspended responsibility. In those carefree days I think I saw only the best aspects of what America had to offer. This time I was here to stay, to raise my son, embark on a new career, and even fall in love. This time I saw America differently.

What I once prized as the mobility of American life now seemed the source of its rootlessness. The friendliness of Americans in their first encounters, their cheerful faces, now often seemed to hide lives of loneliness. Fathers charged their children rent. I knew a mother who enticed her ten-year-old son to steal a document from his father's house so she could use it in court proceedings against him. I knew a woman whose divorce agreement said that she and her wealthy husband would split everything equally—and he went so far as to take volume one of a two-volume English dictionary. I met rich parents who sold their daughters a few bottles of wine. I watched an old lady, cane in hand, take an hour to climb a few steps to her solitary room. I knew lovers who charged one another interest rates. I saw the logic of reciprocity cast its shadow on every human relationship, even love.

Maybe my vision of love is anachronistic, but it was formed by a tradition permeated with mysticism, where self-obliteration in the divine, or in the beloved as the embodiment of the divine, is the goal. In this tradition there are more than a hundred names for different gradations of love, and poets travel easily from the love of the One to the love of the flesh, and find it strange to love anything that smacks of worldliness. It is also a tradition in which the metaphor of love is invariably linked with a sense of melancholy and lamentation.

But here I found a tradition of love where there is little tolerance for melancholy or lamentation, and even less for self-obliteration in the divine. Here, lovers are lonely monads, guarding turfs, who quickly "get on with a new life" when the old love proves impractical. In English, we "fall" in love, whereas in Persian we "become" in love.

One is dangerous and accidental, even serendipitous; the other is transformational and purposeful. Maybe these different conceptions were at the heart of my failed relationship with Barbara.

I am now a permanent exile. I write in both English and Persian. Persian connects me to my past, English is the language of my future. Professional security, never within reach in Iran, has become a reality in the hospitable atmosphere of a small liberal arts college run by the Sisters of Notre Dame. And in spite of my brother's dire predictions, it even proved possible not only to fall in love, but to sustain a satisfying life with an American woman. With Jean, a psychologist whose erudition is complemented by a deep sense of balance and justice and an almost never-ending patience for the irks of living with an exiled, often nostalgic Persian and his teenage son, I might have indeed regained the lost paradise.

──────────── Acknowledgments ────────────

This book has been seven years in the writing. It is not a chronicle of my life but a small collection of its fragments, lived in Tehran and Berkeley in times of turmoil and change.

It was Barbara McDougall more than any one else who convinced me that others might be as interested in these fragments as she was. Her early encouragement and my sorrow when we parted were crucial in the narrative's formative stages.

In a way, anyone who has crossed paths with me over the last forty-six years has helped write this book. Some have, however, played a more active role than others.

Jean Nyland has read and commented on various drafts of the manuscript, providing advice and criticism when the text seemed to require it, and encouragement and comfort when I seemed to need it. She has brought to my life the rare gifts of passionate intensity free from tension, and intellectual challenge mixed with emotional stability. For all of these, I am much indebted to her.

My brothers and sister have been generous with their time, their memories, and their photo albums. Though we shared our childhood, our memories of those days, and our affective responses to them, are at times vastly different.

My brother Hassan offered to read an early draft of the manuscript. His offer, incredible in light of his heavy schedule as a manufacturer, and his keen words afterward, were instrumental in my resolve to continue with the project. As with many other debts I owe him, this one too can never be repaid.

My sister Farzaneh, the soulmate of my childhood years, and the Rock of Gibraltar of my adult life, read and heard various drafts of the book more times than I dare count. She was lavish and kind in her sisterly encouragement, and cautious and insightful in her critical observations.

Parviz Shokat's contributions to this book, and to my life, are beyond words. He is all one could hope for in a friend, and more.

Patricia Andrews, once a student, now a friend, used her wizardry with the computer to produce an early draft of the book.

acknowledgments

I am grateful to the College of Notre Dame for granting me partial leave in Spring 1992 to work on this book and two Faculty Development Grants to continue the project. But more than logistical support, the warmth and quiet of our campus community, the intellectual and emotional support of colleagues, particularly Ardavan Davaran, Sister Pat Hutchison, Kevin Maxwell, Janifer Stackhouse, and Don Stannard-Friel, and finally the avid curiosity of my students about the stories told in this book, have all been essential ingredients in the completion of the manuscript.

Doris Ober edited the book. Her way with words, her sensitivity to the flow of the narrative, and her unhesitant "red-penning" of what she called my "pontifications" and I thought were my deep theoretical musings made the book lighter, the narrative more polished, and the language less encumbered by academic jargon.

I am thankful to Mohammad and Najmieh Batmanglij of Mage Publishers, who spared no effort to make the book, in both form and content, the best it could be.

And last, and most of all, I owe a great debt to my son, Hamid. In many benighted days of my life, he has often been my sole solace.

KODANSHA GLOBE

International in scope, this series offers distinguished books that explore the lives, customs, and mindsets of peoples and cultures around the world.

Other Kodansha Globe titles of interest

JERUSALEM: *Battlegrounds of Memory*
by Amos Elon A dazzling mix of history, geography, travelogue, and memoir. "A word portrait like none of those that have come before of the fabled city. It is from the loving but unsparing pen of Israel's most elegant iconoclast."
—Peter Grose, *The New York Times Book Review* ($14, 1-56836-099-1)

SARAJEVO, EXODUS OF A CITY
by Dzevad Karahasan A Bosnian Muslim intellectual's "biography" of Sarajevo, evoking this cosmopolitan city amid siege and civil war. "A must read for every contemporary person."
— *Die Markische Allgemeine* ($10, 1-56836-057-6)

THE CROSSING PLACE: *A Journey among the Armenians*
by Philip Marsden Caught between warring religions and ideologies, the Armenians have endured and displayed a genius for cultural innovation and survival. "A wonderful journey recounted with knowledge, humour, and a beautiful elegiac sadness."
—*The Observer (London)* ($14, 1-56836-052-5)

OF DREAMS AND DEMONS: *A Memoir of Modern India*
by Patwant Singh "An evocative walk through a life that straddles the best and worst of India's forty-seven independent years."
—Edward W. Desmond, *Time* ($14, 1-56836-086-X)

Please contact your local bookseller for these and other Kodansha titles, or mail your order with payment to:

KODANSHA
Mail Order Department
c/o The Putnam Publishing Group
P.O. Box 12289
Newark, NJ 07101-5289

All orders must be accompanied by payment in full *(check or money order payable to KODANSHA, in U.S. funds only, no cash or C.O.D.s)*, including shipping & handling charges ($3.50 for the first book, $.75 for each additional book). New York State residents please include applicable sales tax. Allow 3–6 weeks for delivery. Prices are subject to change without notice.

When ordering by credit card call **1-800-788-6262**.